"It always seems impossible until it is done."

Nelson Mandela

Published by Panza Publishers

Koppiesvlei 518, Theunissen, 9410

Free State, South Africa

Copyright of text © 2019 Chris Eksteen

Copyright of cover image © 2016 Ingrid Mpofu

All rights reserved.

No part of this publication may be reproduced, distributed, or transmitted in any form or by any means, or stored in a database or retrieval system without the prior written permission of the author.

Edited by Natacha Strauss

Illustrations and cover by Ingrid Mpofu

Printed and bound by Print on Demand in Cape Town, South Africa and CreateSpace in the United States of America, United Kingdom, France, Italy, Japan, New Zealand and Australia.

First edition, first print 2019

ISBN: 978-0-9946935-2-5 (softcover)

ISBN: 978-0-9946935-3-2 (ePub)

ISBN: 978-0-9946935-4-9 (pdf)

Campsite Management and Procedures

Chris Eksteen

Contents

Chapter 1 Business Model, Management and Administration 1

    Standards around the campsite or centre 2

        Stairs 2

        Wheelchair or walking ramps 2

        Table height 2

        Workbench height 2

        Chair height 2

        Coffee table height 2

        Paper sizes 3

        Bunk beds 4

        Keys and locks 4

        Spare keys 5

        Town trip book 5

        Client reminder 5

    Good practice business model 6

    Menu planning 7

    Health and safety 8

        First aid 8

        Record keeping 8

        Needles, sharps and medical waste container 11

        Indemnities 11

        Course reports 13

        Logbook keeping 16

        Health and safety assessment and mediation 16

Emergency evacuation plan 17

Juncture 1: Prevention 24

Juncture 2: Preparedness 26

Emergency planning documents 28

Juncture 3: Response 32

Juncture 4: Recovery 37

Data security 38

Marketing 38

Direct marketing mediums 38

Indirect marketing mediums 40

Notes on marketing to schools 44

Chapter 2 Policies and Procedures 45

Tattoos 46

Piercings 46

Hair policies 46

Pregnancy 47

Sexual orientation and gender identity 47

Clothing policies 47

Relationships 47

Professional relationship and interaction 48

Drugs and alcohol 49

Smoking 49

Criminal records 50

Drinking water policy 50

Swimming pool policy 50

- Sponsors 51
- Snake handling equipment 52
- Chapter 3 Saving Resources and Self-help 52
  - Snake hook 54
  - Snake tubes 54
- Tips on water saving 55
  - Toilets 55
  - Water-saving showerheads 55
  - Tap aerators 56
  - Gardens 56
  - Irrigation 56
  - Leaks 56
  - Pipe isolation 57
- Tips for energy saving 57
  - Motion sensor lights 57
  - Geyser blankets 57
  - Geyser timers 58
  - Solar geyser 58
- Upcycling around the centre 59
  - Tyre chairs 59
  - Tyre dog house 59
  - Soccer goal posts 60
- Saving resources 60
  - Saving in the kitchen 60
  - Paintball tip 61

- Fire hydrants lockable cases 61
- Trailer sockets 62

Chapter 4 Basics on Maintenance 62

- Electrical plugs 65
- Distribution boxes 66
- Geyser and solar geyser explained 67
- How to reverse a door lock 68
- Basic toolbox 68
- How to fix a burst copper water pipe 69
- PVC drain pipes 70
- How to fix a leaky tap 70
- How to join a power cord 71
- How to check for air or gas leaks 71
- How to get a 45-degree angle 72
- Septic tanks 72
- Testing battery life 74
- Campfire site tips 74
- Fence fixing tips 74
- Producing a two- or three-strand wire tip 75
- How to mix concrete 76
- Replacing old roof nails with new screws 77
- Traditional Drilling VS Hammer drilling 77
- Different drill bits 78
- Prolonging the life of a drill bit 80
- How to install a window 81

Photo Credits 82

PREFACE

In this second book of the *'Outdoor Education Resource Series'*, I hope to provide industry newcomers with a starting point in campsite management and also trust that it will be helpful to those with years of experience. While it is almost impossible to cover all aspects of management in this unique and ever-changing industry, this book will certainly put one on the right track.

This book is dedicated to my wife, Delana and my two sons, Hendrik C Ostwald and Christiaan Isaac Eksteen. They are my world.

Last, but certainly not least, I would like to thank all of my readers and followers. Without you, this series would not have seen the light of day. Thank you!

Regards

Chris Eksteen

2019

CHAPTER 1
BUSINESS MODEL, MANAGEMENT AND ADMINISTRATION

Standards around the campsite or centre

Stairs

Step height typically ranges between 15 cm to 18 cm and width between 28 cm and 30 cm – 15 cm x 30 cm being the easiest configuration to use for maximum comfort. It is however more important that all the steps in the staircase be of equal size. Rule of thumb: 25 cm is the maximum height for a rostrum before you need to add additional steps.

Wheelchair or walking ramps

The maximum ramp slope is 1:10, though it is still rather steep and most ramps in practice are 1:12+. The latter means that for every one metre you want to go up, you need 12 metres of ramp to get to that height.

Table height

A dining or writing table's standard height is 760 mm.

Workbench height

A common workbench height is 900 mm. This is important for your kitchen and other working benches as a lower working surface causes fatigue and back pain.

Chair height

A dining chair's standard height is 500 mm and works well with the standard table height of 760 mm (See above).

Coffee table height

A coffee table's height is the same as a soft chair or couch, 400 mm.

Paper sizes

Refer to the chart below to see the paper sizes in comparison.

Paper size	Width in mm	Length in mm
A0	841	1189
A1	594	841
A2	420	594
A3	297	420
A4	210	297
A5	148	210
A6	105	148
A7	74	105
A8	52	74
US Letter	216	279
US Legal	216	356

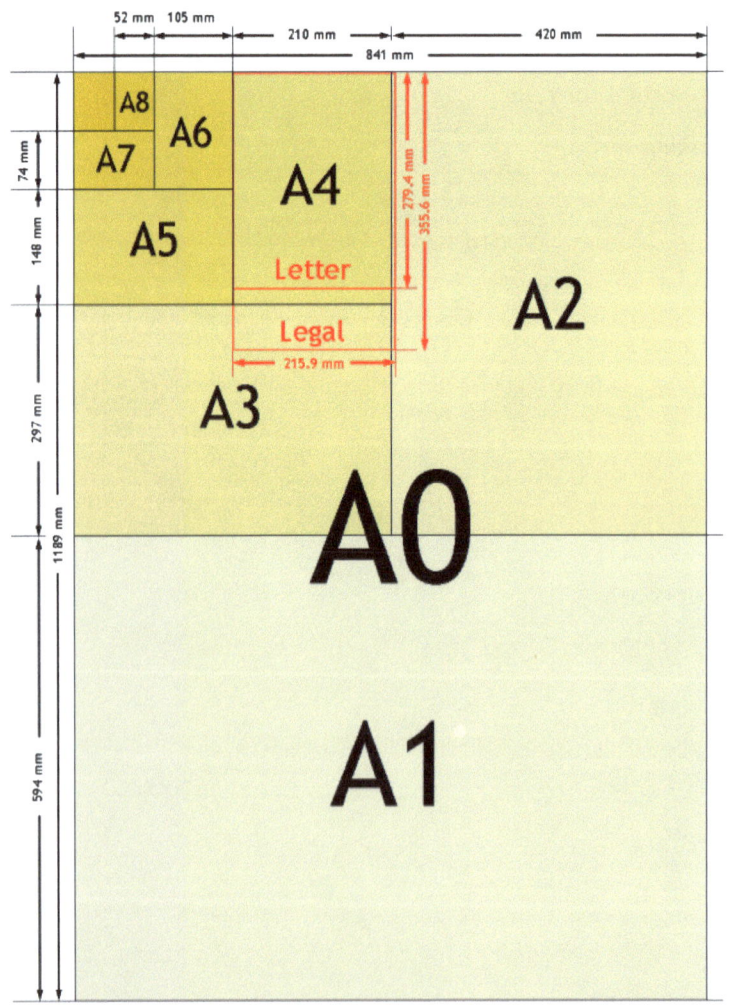

Bunk beds

Bunk beds, double or triple stacked, are often used at campsites.

Guard railings are essential to prevent children from falling out of bed. Sometimes quarter or half-length railings are used to save money on construction, but full-length guards are the safest and should be considered.

Since bunk bed sizes vary, it can be difficult to find bedding such as fitted sheets. To save money, you can purchase rolls of material and make your own sheets.

Mattresses should also be covered with a canvas or waterproof material to prolong lifespan, whether you choose foam or spring mattresses.

Campsites often provide sheets with their beds, even if campers bring their own bedding, as this basic measure protects mattresses from spills and dirt.

Keys and locks

Emergency keys need to be placed in suitable containers at all main exits. These key boxes normally have a breakable glass front so that the key can be accessed in case of an emergency. Children often fiddle with these key boxes and try to access the keys. Some key boxes have screws that keep the frame in place but once the screws are loosened and removed the glass and frame can shift to expose the key. It is useful to glue these frames in place or to use silicone to secure the glass. Some emergency key boxes have an alarm connected to them and should the glass be broken, or key removed, the alarm will sound. Some doors also have keyless emergency handles to facilitate an easy exit in case of an emergency. Normally these doors also sound an alarm when opened.

Many campsites charge a fee for boxes or seals broken by campers when there is no emergency.

Spare keys

All spare keys must be locked away in a safe place. It is a good idea to also have a list of all lockable doors with their respective reference numbers so a new key can be cut in case the original and spare keys are lost. This exercise also indicates which doors perhaps share the same key.

Town trip book

Many campsites and centres are remote. It is, therefore, good practice to have a book in a central place or office where a list can be made of things that need to either be picked up, dropped off or purchased with a trip to town. This becomes very handy when planning a trip to town or laying out a route for a trip. It also aids in budgeting for things needed. The main reason to keep a book in a central place is because one can simply not remember everything that is needed for a centre or campsite and having all staff contributing to this activity saves time and money.

Client reminder

Clients often need reminding of things such as sharing special dietary requirements and final numbers. This can be done by developing either an automated or manual system for sending clients an email one month before arrival and again 14 days before arrival.

The first email, sent one month before arrival, can contain maps and directions to the campsite (so they can book or plan transport), indemnity forms, the menu, a programme, camp rules and invoice for deposit (if not requested at the time of booking).

The second email, sent 14 days before arrival, could remind the client to send final numbers for the camp including a boy-girl ratio, ask for special dietary requirements and remind recipients of indemnity forms that need to be filled out by parents and the school.

Good practice business model

Many campsites and centres have their own model on how they do or foresee to do business. Conducting business under a personal name carries risks and exposes you as an individual to possible claims, lawsuits and debt. When you conduct business under a private company, trust or corporation you give the business a legal entity which in many cases accepts all or most of the liability. However, as an owner, director or board you can still be held accountable for negligence. Still, as a corporate entity, you also enjoy tax benefits and can sometimes get better rates on bank fees and administration costs.

A good business model has multiple companies or entities running different sections of your site. An example of this is to have a main entity running the day-to-day business, the one functioning as the face of the organisation. *This is where your public liability will lie and under which name professional indemnity insurance is taken out on*. A second company or entity manages investments and assets such as property, buildings, etc *This entity will rent out the facilities to the main entity.* A third company or entity is in charge of equipment such as vehicles and will rent out equipment to the main entity. This approach not only helps with the splitting of income and tax but also aids in liability and insurance matters. This way should something tragic happen to your organisation, you will not lose your assets or equipment as they are not in the liability bearing entity.

Some sites and centres even split their business activities, for example, one entity runs the camps and activities and a second manages the catering as this again splits the income and affects taxation.

It is important that you do not take on activities with the possibility of liability, like taking out loans or contracts in the same entity than your assists as this will defeat the purpose of safeguarding assets in said entity.

It is important to discuss your needs with your accountant who can help you choose a model that will work for you. After all, no two businesses are alike.

Menu planning

When creating menus for a camp, whether it is a permanent, weekly or group-specific menu, it is important to keep cost in mind while delivering quality, balanced meals. Make sure you know what each meal costs – including ingredients, cooking and labour – so you can stay within budget when creating menus.

When doing menu planning, ensure that you take the whole menu into consideration. You may find that, for example, day one and day two are perfectly balanced on their own but if both days feature potatoes and chicken in some form you could, for example, swap day two with day three. Variety is important to keep your menus interesting and clients happy. Budget-friendly menus need not be dull and boring. Even camp food, planned properly, can be fit for a king.

An example of a five meal weekend menu compiled from book one in this book series *"Cooking for a Camp, Hostel or Large Group"* can be seen below. (Page numbers are indicated for reference to *"Cooking for a Camp, Hostel or Large Group)*

	Friday	Saturday	Sunday
BREAKFAST		Oats (p.9) Eggs (p.13) Tomato (p.14) Mushrooms (p.14) Toasted Bread (p.15)	Cereals (p.11) Yoghurt (p.20) and Muesli French Toast (p.15) Cheese + Syrup
LUNCH		Macaroni + Cheese (p.23) Coleslaw (p.55) Fruit	Hotdogs (p.24) Sauce (p.43) & Chips (p.23) Fruit
DINNER	Lasagne (p.28) Rolls Mixed Vegetables (p.50) Chocolate Cake (p.68)	Chicken Pie (p.36) Pumpkin Fritters (p.47) Salad Malva Pudding (p.71) & Custard (p.68)	

Health and safety

First aid

All staff must be trained in basic first aid and CPR. Rules regarding CPR and first aid change all the time and it is management's responsibility to ensure training is up to date.

A few things to remember:

As far as possible, do not allow male on female and vice versa first aid. Never treat a person alone. Instead, ask another staff member, teacher or client to be present.

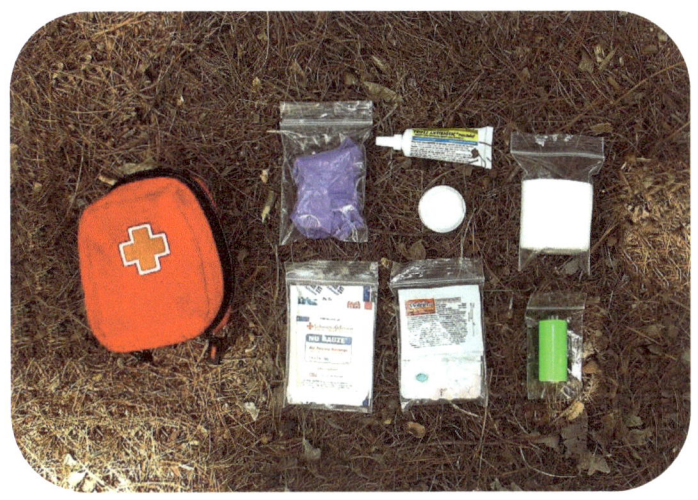

A good rule of thumb for safe first aid administration: Do not take out, put in or slice.

In a nutshell: You are not allowed to give medication or injections.

Please note: There are things such as Do Not Resuscitate (DNR) tattoos and bracelets that exist in several forms. This 'restricts' you from resuscitating a person, however, 'Do Not Resuscitate' does not mean do not help or treat. You must still do whatever you can to help the person. Many responders, doctors and medical staff insist on having a medical certificate stating, 'Do Not Resuscitate'. Without said certificate, they ignore bracelets and tattoos as these are not legally binding in most countries.

Record keeping

It is vital that your first aiders keep a record of whom they treat and the treatments provided. This can help to track what first aid stock was used and to identify patterns or problem areas where incidents keep occurring so that the cause can be addressed.

Here is an example of such a report that can be kept in first aid packs. These reports should be filed for safekeeping.

FIRST-AID FIELD KIT REPORT

Date: _____

First-aider:

Name: _____

Telephone no: _____

Signature: _____

Casualty:

Name: _____

School: _____

Telephone no: _____

Male/Female   Age: _____

Incident:

Type of incident: _____

First Aid Given:

_____
_____
_____

Another record that needs to be kept is a stocktake of first-aid packs. Before a group arrives, or at least once a week, the boxes, kits and packs should be checked and stock needs to be refilled where necessary.

You can have a customised list for each first-aid box, kit or pack. These stock reports form part of your health and safety practices on how to ensure safety for your employees and clients.

Weekly first-aid stock take – field pack

		DATE:						
10	Adhesive Plaster							
10	Gauze Swabs							
2	Bandages (100mm x 4.5m)							
1	Tweezers							
4	Safety Pins							
10	Gloves							
1	Scissor							
2	Disposable Triangular Bandages							
1	Ring Pad							
1	Sterile Dressing (No 5)							
1	Sterile Dressing (No 3)							
1	Eye Pad with a Bandage							
1	75ml Antiseptic Cream							
1	Roller Plaster							
1	Hypoallergenic Plaster							
1	CPR Mouthpiece							
2	Splints							
1	Burn Gel 50ml							
1	Glucose Gel							
1	Sanitary Pad							
4	Sterile Needles							
2	Allergy Tablets							
2	Eyedrops							
1	Hand Sanitiser Spray							
1	Digital Thermometer (Check Battery)							
1	Medical Waste Bag							
1	Sharps Waste Bag							
1	First-aid Report A5							
5	First-aid Reports A6							

Kit No. ___

***File when completed.   Sign: _____

Needles, sharps and medical waste container

It is essential to have a small container in each first-aid pack for the disposal of all sharps (such as needles) and medical waste (such as plasters). These small containers can then be emptied or transferred into bigger designated sharps and medical waste containers. These containers need to be discarded in accordance with your country's legislation. In many areas, there are companies that sell containers and replace them once full. Ask local doctors, clinics or hospitals for preferred suppliers in the area. These containers normally have a closed lid (with a small opening for depositing hazardous content) to prevent contamination. Keep these containers in a safe spot.

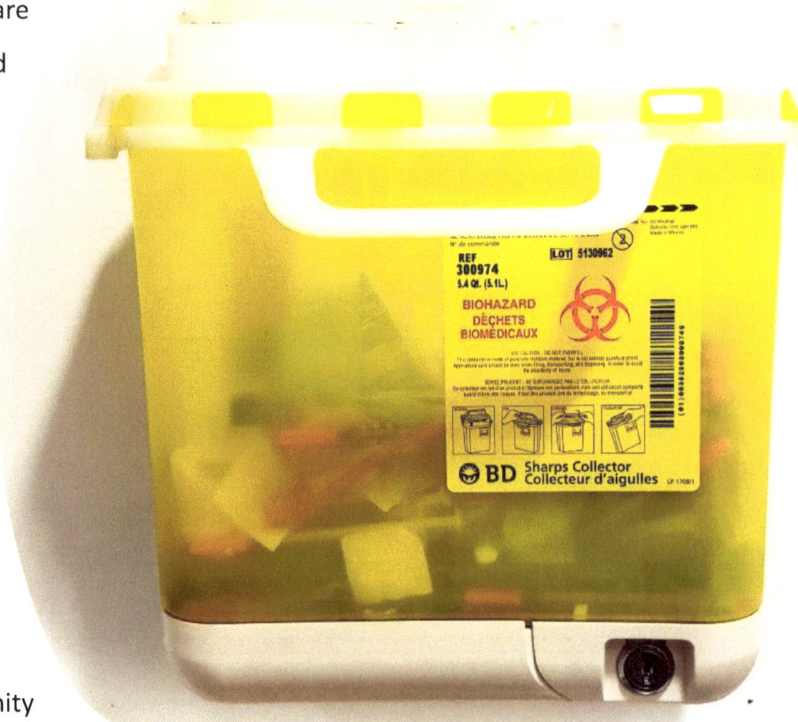

Indemnities

Ensure that you update your indemnity agreements regularly and make the latest versions available on your website. Also, identify a dedicated storage space for documents and inform your staff. After each programme, the related indemnity agreements should be archived to make space for the new group's documentation.

TIP for photo and video indemnity insurance: You need to reserve the right to use photos and videos taken at your centre for the purpose of advertising or social media. Should you not have permission, you need to ensure that those photos and videos are not used or stored for later use.

Here is an example of an indemnity form:

NB: Please ensure that the Medical Details section is correctly completed.

Personal details

School / group name: _____

Child's full names: _____

Parent's full names: _____

Parent's / guardian's phone numbers:
_____
_____

Medical aid scheme: _____
Medical aid number: _____
Medical aid phone number: _____

Please attach a front and back copy of your medical card.

Doctor's name: _____
Phone number: _____

Dietary requirements (if any): _____

Allergies: _____

Recent illness or other medical conditions: _____
_____

Can your child swim confidently in deep water? _____

Please note: In case of emergency, participants will be removed by road (or air if necessary) to the nearest appropriate medical facility in the following towns..................

Consent & indemnity

I, _____, (parent/guardian/self) make application for my child/ward/self _____ to participate in an excursion to COMPANY / CAMPSITE NAME. I fully understand and accept date of birth _____

that this excursion will be undertaken at my child's/ward's/own risk and I undertake on behalf of myself/my executors, my spouse and my child/ward/self aforesaid, to indemnify, absolve and hold blameless COMPANY / CAMPSITE NAME and all other persons and organisations associated with the trail/hike/excursion against and from all claims whatsoever that may arise in connection with the loss of, or damage to the property, or injury to the person of my child/ward/self aforesaid in the course of the trail/hike/excursion.

I accept the following conditions:
My child/ward/self will abide by the instructions of those in charge of the party.

1. My child/ward/self is/am physically fit and able to undertake strenuous exercise.
2. That I fully informed those in charge of the party of any allergies/special dietary needs/medical conditions/recent illnesses on this form.
3. Any photos and/or videos and/or recordings made on the camp may be used on our website and in marketing material.
4. I will not send junk food/takeaways with my child/ward to camp as I know this carries a potential risk of food poisoning.
5. I will ensure my child/ward does not take any dangerous goods such as weapons/fireworks/ crackers and/or any drugs/alcohol/cigarettes/tobacco to camp.
6. A set of camp rules are available on our website www._____. It will be the responsibility of me as parent/guardian/self to arrange for immediate pickup in the case of expulsion due to rules not followed.

Your safety is **our priority** but also **your responsibility**.

Signature of one or more parent/guardian necessary if participant is under the age of 21.

1 _____
2 _____

Course reports

Two reports are important for collecting information on how a camp was experienced by clients and staff.

1. A client's report allows clients to share how they experienced your centre and provides them with an opportunity to inform you of concerns or things that need to be fixed.
2. A staff report outlines things that went wrong or right, allowing for reflection on the programme and providing an opportunity to fix mistakes. In short: Problem areas and safety risks that need attention can be identified and addressed. Incidents can also be reported here for record keeping.

Again, these records form part of your health and safety measures and can highlight a pattern or problem area. Examples of course reports.

TEACHER / GROUP LEADER COURSE ASSESSMENT

Organising teacher: _____ Date of course: _____

School: _____ Grade/Group: _____

Other teachers: _____

Please help us to make sure we have your updated contact details:

Postal address: _____ Code: _____

Best time to call: _____ Email address: _____

Please be honest as your comments help us to improve – thank you!

PROGRAMME CONTENT (relevance, level, accessibility):

WHAT WOULD YOU LIKE TO SEE ADDED TO THE PROGRAMME?

STAFF CAPABILITIES (please comment on style, appearance, techniques, professionalism):

MEALS:

FACILITIES (cleanliness, maintenance, etc.):

COMMENTS & IDEAS:

Signed (teacher in charge): _____

COURSE REPORT (to be filled out by camp staff)

School: _____ Date of course: _____

Teacher in charge: _____ Grade/Group: _____

Other teachers: _____

Course theme: _____ Staff in charge: _____

Other staff: _____

PROGRAMME: What worked and why?

What didn't work and why:

LOGISTICS & PLANNING: Any hiccups?

STAFF CAPABILITIES: How did we do as a team?

MEALS:

COMMENTS FOR NEXT GROUP (comments re. unique group characteristics, special requests, needs & interests):

EVALUATION (score out of 10):

Staff communication ____   Staff enthusiasm ____   Programme quality ____

Dealing with problems ____   Weather ____   Smooth running ____   Overall feelings ____

Signed: Activity leader in charge: _____

Logbook keeping

Keeping a logbook, wherein equipment is recorded and the use of items are tracked, is essential.

Ropes and adventure gear need logging to indicate when they have to be retired after prolonged use.

Fire extinguishers need to be serviced at the recommended intervals and thus require logging.

Vehicles need logbooks for tracking services, tyre replacement and fuel consumption.

Warranty documents for all equipment and appliances bought should be logged. Here you can keep a copy of the invoice along with manuals and repair receipts.

Maintenance logbooks show the maintenance team what needs to be done and what has already been done and by whom. They also indicate patterns in maintenance and breakdown. In addition, staff can use maintenance logbooks to report damages or breakages to the maintenance team.

Training logbooks are used to record training provided and details of the recipients to see which team members still need training and in which areas or fields they need it.

Emergency drill logbooks contain the details of monthly emergency drill exercises to prove they were carried out and to log what went wrong, how long it took and improvement is required.

All logbooks form part of your health and safety activities.

Health and safety assessment and mediation

It is the responsibility of all staff to help with the assessment of health and safety risks. Set a schedule and go through the whole site, reports and logbooks to identify potential threats and hazards and to determine how they can be fixed or prevented.

A few examples of what can be found on a check and what should be included in your health and safety monthly report:

- Obstacle course: Reports on the previous two groups state that two children were hurt on the obstacle course in separate cases. Both obtained cuts from a loose wire.

    Inspected the obstacle course: Found wire sticking out from a worn cable.

    Maintenance is informed and instructed to fix it before the new group arrives.

- Staircase: The inspection revealed that one of the steps on the concrete staircase to the second storey is uneven and slightly wider than the others. It could cause someone to trip and fall.

  The problem was reported to management and the maintenance team.

  Solution:

  The budget could not accommodate reconstruction of the staircase, but the following was done:

  Reconstructing the staircase was placed on a to-do list for when the budget would allow it. A sign was made to warn people that the steps are uneven and that they should hold on to the railing. The step in question was painted red and an anti-slip guard was placed on the edge of the step.

- Rabbits dug a hole by the amphitheatre's gate. To prevent injury, the hole was filled with soil.

Emergency evacuation plan

Each room must have an emergency exit and a notice of the emergency route one should follow to the nearest emergency assembly point. These notices can be placed on the back of the door or near the door or light switch.

Keep a copy of records outlining all emergency exits, routes and maps.

Some examples of a collective emergency exit route plan:

Emergency map

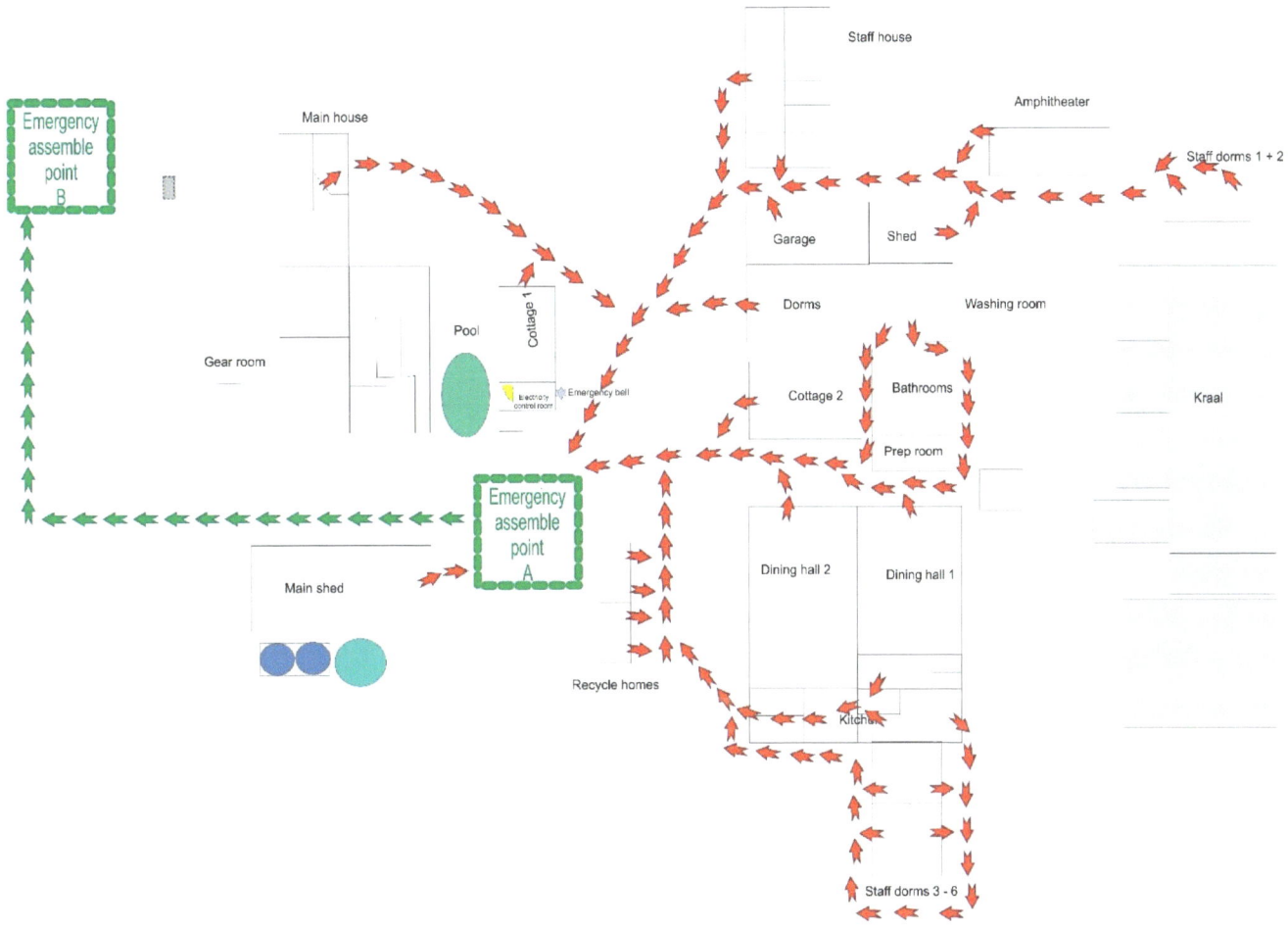

It is important to have an electricity and a water map of your site. These should be kept in your office and handed over to emergency respondents upon their arrival. Online backups are recommended as well.

It is good practice to keep a file with your emergency exit routes, electrical map, water map and emergency procedures at your main first-aid station or in your emergency room.

Electricity maps can also be affixed to each distribution box or placed in your electricity supply room.

Here are examples of electricity and water maps.

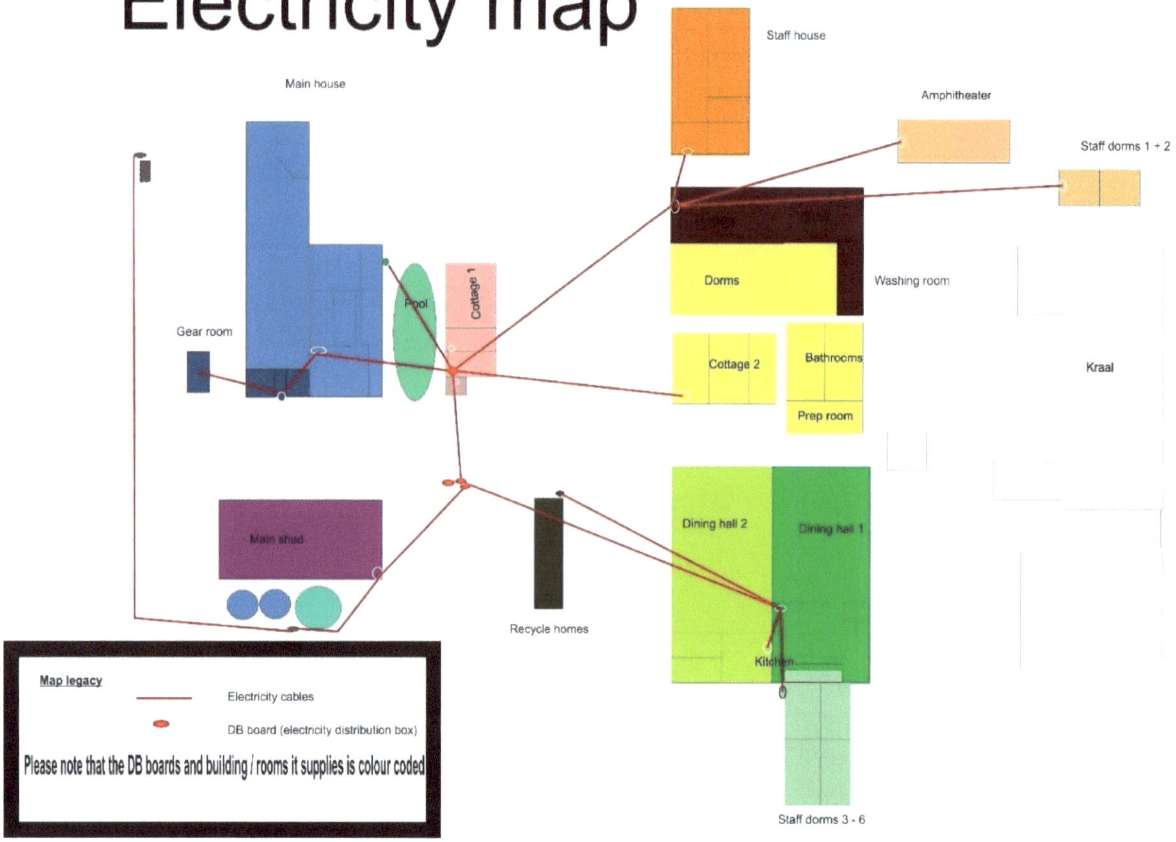

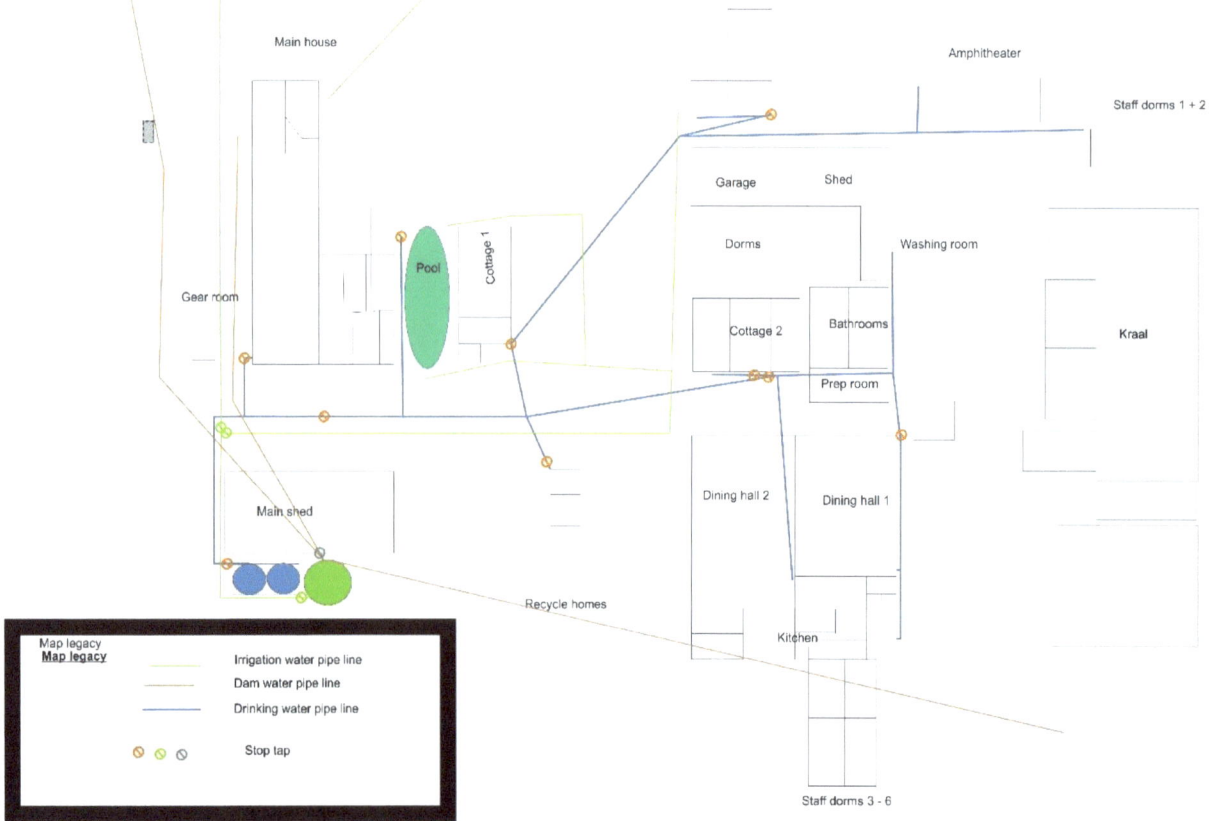

Emergencies as a topic is unpleasant to discuss, but it is a very important part of managing a centre or campsite.

No two emergency plans will look the same as every site is unique. It is vitally important that you identify your problem areas and design an emergency plan/protocol to address them.

This list of items you intend to fix must be updated from time to time showing dates along with problem areas addressed and problems fixed. This is very important as it shows intent. When it comes to the law of negligence, you will have a much stronger case if you can show intent on fixing things and reasons why other problem areas have not been fixed. Whether there are financial, staff or knowledge constraints, add the details in your plan. That said, you cannot hide behind a list of intent. You have to address the problem areas and prioritise as and when your budget, time and workforce allow.

Few things to remember regarding your campsite emergency plan:

An emergency drill schedule and logbook need to be kept (and keep a copy of the logbook with your emergency kit).

Management needs to set a drill schedule and execute it on the scheduled dates and times. It is important to test scenarios and staff should not be informed beforehand of a scheduled drill so the test can be authentic and useful.

Example of an emergency drill log:

Monthly	Date conducted	Group	Weather	Number of participants	Evacuation time	Comments

Ensure that you revise your plan every year as things might change, for example, phone numbers.

Keep track of the revisions on the front page of your camp's emergency plan to show that you consciously intended to keep your attendees safe by updating your emergency plan (see page 23).

Example of a revision record table that can be included in the emergency plan:

Revision record:			
VERSION	DATE REVISED	AMENDED BY	APPROVED BY

It is also recommended that you test all the emergency numbers to ensure you have the correct ones to request the relevant emergency services.

It is very important that you do the following when conducting test calls:

- ❖ Identify yourself and your site
- ❖ Explain that it is a drill and that you are testing your list of emergency numbers
- ❖ Ask if they can talk to you now
- ❖ Ask your questions and keep it brief

In some countries, all the emergency help is centralised. For example, in the United States of America, 911 is the standard number for all emergency services and it works throughout the country.

If your country does not have a centralised emergency helpline, ensure that you have your local emergency numbers documented. These can include but are not limited to:

Air ambulance	Clinic	Hospital	Search and rescue
Ambulance	Counsellors / psychologist	Immigration control	Traffic
Bomb squad	Doctor	Neighbours	Wildlife control
Chemist	Drug and poison centre	Police	
Churches	Fire department	Rehab centre	

Emergency numbers should be placed not only in your emergency plan but also in prominent areas, such as your kitchen, office, main halls and by first-aid kits.

Ensure that a copy of the emergency plan is kept in your office and also added to your emergency kit at a central location.

Example of emergency kit contents:

- Emergency numbers
- First-aid kit
- Fire extinguisher
- Emergency blanket
- Whistles
- Bell (cow/sheep bell works well)
- Copy of camp emergency plan
- Pencils
- Writing paper
- Rubber bands and cards or key rings to mark casualties
- Map of the site showing where all buildings are located
- Basic electricity map showing each building's power source and locations of distribution boxes
- Basic water map showing each building's water source and locations of all the stop taps
- Basic gas plan showing which buildings have gas and where the shut-off valves are located
- Escape routes
- Incident reports
- Child release forms
- Drill logbook
- Flashlights
- Local telephone directory
- Lists of other emergency responders phone numbers

It is advised that a letter and copy of your camp's emergency plan/protocol is sent to your local doctors, hospitals, fire- and police departments. The letter can ask for their input and any changes or advice that relate to your plan. It is further advised that you get a signed receipt acknowledgement letter from these parties. This proves that the plan has been made available to them and that you are committed to ensuring the safest site for your attendees whether staff or client. Here follows an example of a campsite emergency plan that can easily be adapted to address your needs:

DESCRIPTION

OUR CAMPSITE EMERGENCY PLAN

This emergency management plan describes _____ campsite and its environment, the potential hazards to which it is likely to be exposed and the manner in which the campsite will manage emergencies.

This campsite emergency plan/protocol is an improving and growing document.

This plan is set out to show the role of all individuals on site in case of an emergency.

A copy of the campsite emergency plan will be available in the office. The plan also forms part of the staff training and will be given to each staff member.

Our campsite emergency plan is also available on the camp's website.

This emergency plan is divided into four phases:

Juncture 1 - Prevention

Juncture 2 – Preparedness

Juncture 3 – Response

Juncture 4 - Recovery

Revision record:			
VERSION	DATE REVISED	AMENDED BY	APPROVED BY

Juncture 1: Prevention

PREVENTION refers to the steps/actions taken by the site to lower the risk and odds of an emergency occurring.

It also looks at the steps/actions taken by the site to reduce the impact of an emergency that cannot be prevented beforehand.

Prevention sits at the core of running a campsite. Being proactive in areas of concern, rather than reacting when emergencies occur, can save lives and reduce damage to property.

This is where you list all the steps the campsite takes to be proactive and prevent an emergency from occurring.

Examples of basic steps a campsite can take to be proactive:

Development a camp emergency plan.

Train staff in CPR, first aid, firefighting and emergencies.

Communicate changes to the plan to all role players.

Draw up of building-, electricity-, water- and gas plans of the campsite.

Submit the camp emergency plan to key role players such as the fire department, hospitals, doctors and police.

Review the camp emergency plan regularly.

Review all accidents that happened on the site and work on solutions to prevent them in the future.

Practise emergency drills.

Test emergency numbers.

Place warning signs at high-risk areas (for example workshop, chemical storage, flammable liquids, excavation).

It is good practice to have staff check the campsite regularly to look for possible hazards. Here are a few examples of hazardous areas and preventative measures taken during and after routine inspections:

- Place railings on bunk beds
- Cover drains with concrete slabs
- Identify no-go zones and mark them clearly
- Mark steps and equip them with anti-slip strips
- Sand down sharp edges
- Tighten loose wires on the obstacle course
- Install a water pipe to the campfire area
- Service fire extinguishers
- Install emergency keys
- Place emergency numbers at all main doors
- Put an electrical and water map in each electrical distribution box
- Have emergency route maps at each main door
- Fix loose carpet in the room
- Fix broken windows
- Enclose open electrical sockets
- Mark non-potable water taps

Keep records of these inspections and the problem areas identified. Also, put dates next to the items fixed or problems solved to show the progress in making the campsite safer. Items in the emergency toolbox should not be used for anything other than emergency and preparedness training activities. An assigned Emergency Response Team member should be responsible for keeping the toolbox updated (change batteries, update phone numbers, etc.). The toolbox should be portable and readily accessible for use in an emergency. Contents of an Emergency toolbox is discussed earlier in this section.

Juncture 2: Preparedness

PREPAREDNESS refers to outlining what you will do in the event of an accident or emergency before it occurs.

Preparedness activities:

Prepare first-aid kits   Practise emergency drills

Prepare emergency toolkits   Test emergency numbers

It is good practice to identify a campsite emergency response team to act in case of emergency.

Internal participants could be:

Camp director

Camp manager

Activity guides/educators

Support staff (kitchen en grounds)

External participants could be:

Health professionals

Police

Fireteam

Community

Responsibilities of each person on the emergency team:

Camp director

The director will generally serve as chief in command and will be responsible for delegating tasks and overseeing all processes during an emergency.

Responsibilities include:

Taking all steps and implementing emergency protocols to ensure the safety of staff, campers and visitors on site.

Assisting emergency personnel including doctors, fire department, search and rescue or police with information.

Providing maps, charts and headcounts to emergency personnel.

Activating the rest of the campsite emergency response team.

Representing the camp and speaking to the media.

Maintaining communication with the relevant authorities, schools and parents.

Manager

The manager shall serve as chief in command when the director is not available and otherwise support the director in his/her duties as set out above.

Educators/guides

Educators shall be responsible for the supervision of learners/campers and shall remain with them until directed otherwise.

They shall:

Take steps deemed necessary to ensure the safety of learners, staff and other individuals during the implementation of the protocols.

Render first aid if and where necessary.

Report missing learners and staff to the director.

Assist as directed by the chief commander.

Support/ground staff

Survey and report damage to the chief commander.

Control main shut-off valves for gas, water and electricity.

Assist as directed by the chief commander.

All external participants

Assist as directed by the chief commander.

Emergency planning documents
This document can help with the development of the camp emergency plan and in planning and preparing for an emergency.

1. Staff skills inventory
2. Details of the campsite emergency response team members
3. Learners/staff with special needs
4. Designated assembly area 1 — outdoors (for standard evacuation)
5. Designated assembly area 2 — alternate building location A: within walking distance
6. Designated assembly area 3 — alternate building location B: requiring transport
7. Roll call and release

1. **Staff skills inventory**

Make a list of all the staff members, their skills and training received. This will assist in knowing who can help in different situations. Skills could include but are not limited to:

1. First aid
2. CPR
3. Firefighting
4. Snake handling
5. Spider and scorpion handling
6. Multilingual
7. Radio Experience

2. **Campsite emergency response team members**

Name	Role	Phone number	Radio call
XXXXXXX	DIRECTOR	08X 44X 0X13	CHRIS
XXXXXXX	MANAGER	08X 70X 6X65	AMI
XXXXXXX	GUIDE	08X 59X 4X88	JOHN

3. **Learners/staff with special needs**

During a welcoming tea, the camp director or manager will give teachers and group leaders a list of all children and group members with special needs.

Group leaders then review indemnity forms to look for notes from parents regarding special/medical needs and then compile a list. All team leaders are then notified of special needs and if there are dietary requirements, the kitchen is notified. The special needs list is placed with the indemnity forms in a designated place for easy access.

4. **Designated assembly area 1 — outdoors (for standard evacuation)**

Identify an emergency assembly area outdoors where learners will have minimal exposure to dangers or hazards around the camp. Also, select a second area should the first become unsafe. Then allocate space for each of the following at each assembly area:

Command post – preferably an elevated area

Access for emergency vehicles

Learner assembly areas

First-aid area

Psychological counselling area

Potential temporary mortuary

Post the heliport GPS coordinates and emergency information (including numbers) next to the assembly board.

5. **Designated assembly area 2 — alternate building location A: walking distance**

In case of inclement weather, a building within walking distance might be better suited than the typical outdoor assembly area.

From the outdoor assembly areas, groups can be moved to safer buildings until further arrangements can be made. This could include areas like a shed, dining halls or dorms.

6. **Designated assembly area 3 — alternate building location B: requiring transport**

In severe cases, transport will be required to evacuate learners and staff to an off-site building or location, for example, if there is a large fire.

This area should be identified beforehand and the necessary arrangements made. Feature the contact details of the identified facility on the form and provide a map that can be handed to the drivers who will evacuate the groups from the campsite.

As with the standard assembly area, the following have to be identified:

Command post – preferably an elevated area	First-aid area
Access for emergency vehicles	Psychological counselling area
Learner assembly areas	Potential temporary mortuary

7. Roll call & release

Each group leader must carry out headcounts to ensure all members are accounted for.

Any missing person will be reported to senior personnel.

No child may be released to a parent or guardian without the knowledge of the group leader/teacher and senior personnel. A form also needs to be signed before a child is handed to a parent or guardian in order to keep track of children leaving the campsite and to have the details of the person collecting the child.

Keep the release forms with the indemnity forms.

Juncture 3: Response

RESPONSE is the implementation of a plan once an incident occurs. A list of emergency response protocols should be drawn up and planned for in advance.

These emergencies could include but are not limited to:

Accidents at camp	Hostage situation
Allergic reaction	Kidnapping
Assault	Lockdown
Bomb threat	Narcotic abuse
Chemical material spill	Missing person
Death or serious illness	Poisoning
Drop, cover & hold	Rape / sexual abuse
Drowning	Power outage
Earthquake	School bus accident
Evacuation	Suicide
Extreme weather	Threat of violence
Fire	Trespasser/intruder
HIV / AIDS infection	Weapons

Here are a few examples of how emergency protocols can be structured to suit the needs of a campsite/centre. It is important to develop protocols that will be effective in your environment and to update them as one will see what works and what does not work in different situations. It is important to note that, even though protocols are written and developed to be thorough and to serve as a guideline, more or even other actions might be needed than what is stipulated. This is because each situation will be unique and each event produces unique circumstances. No two emergencies are the same.

ACCIDENTS AT CAMP

Staff actions for minor events:
- Provide for immediate medical attention, "first aid"
- Report the accident to management

Staff actions for major events:
- Report the accident to the director or main administration office
- Inform medical support
- Provide for immediate medical attention including performing necessary life-sustaining measures if needed (CPR, AED, etc.), until emergency medical services arrive.

Director / response team actions:
- Provide appropriate medical attention and call emergency medical services if necessary
- Inform the head of the campsite emergency response team of the incident
- Contact the parents/guardian of the learner to report the incident and seek further instructions
- Complete an incident report and appropriate documentation

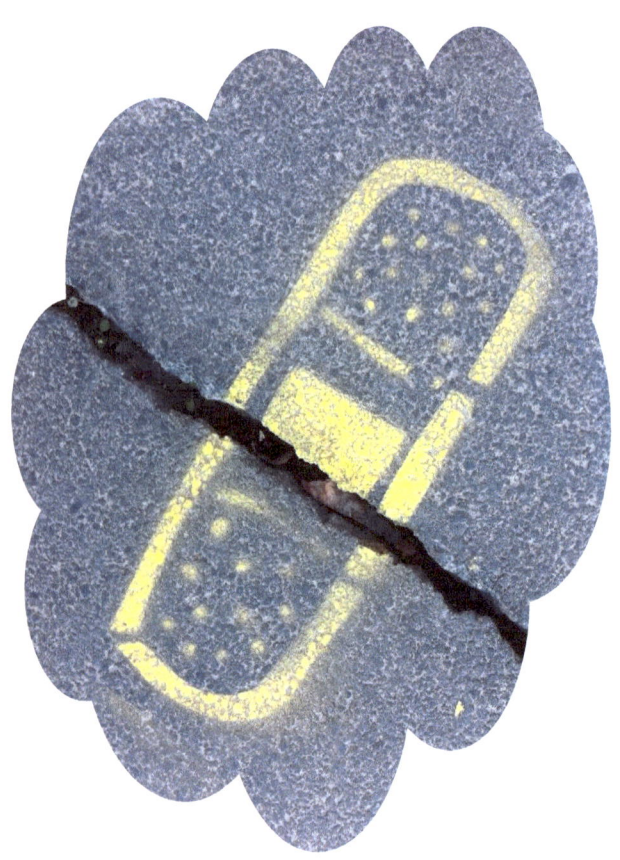

ALLERGIC REACTION

Possible symptoms:

- Skin irritation or itching, rash, hives, nasal itching, sneezing, localised swelling, swollen tongue
- Restlessness, sweating, fright, shock
- Shortness of breath, vomiting, cough, hoarseness

Staff actions:

- If the learner is in imminent danger, notify the director and send for immediate help (first aid, CPR, emergency medical services) and the first aid kit
- Assist in getting any medication (such as epinephrine) prescribed for the learner (usually kept in the learner's backpack or main office)
- Keep the learner comfortable
- Move the learner only for safety reasons

Director / response team actions:

- Call emergency medical services if deemed necessary
- Administer appropriate medical assistance, such as:

    Provide medication as directed by a physician

    Apply an ice pack to the affected area

    Keep the patient warm

    Watch closely for respiratory difficulty and be prepared to respond with oxygen

- Notify the campsite emergency response team
- Notify the learner's parents/guardian of the incident
- Record all details relating to the incident, for example, time and site of an insect sting; food ingested; the name of medicine, dosage and time administered, etc.

FIRE

Staff actions:

- Sound the fire alarm
- Call the director and provide details of the location and extent of the fire
- Implement evacuation procedures to an outside assembly area
- Implement the emergency plan for any learners needing special assistance
- Follow standard — learner roll call procedures
- Do not re-enter the building until given the all clear by the director or campsite emergency response team
- Determine if arrangements need to be made for transportation to an alternate building or location, or if the camp is to be dismissed

Director / response team actions:

- Call the fire department
- Activate the campsite emergency response team
- Establish whether any learners or staff have been injured or are missing
- Call the police and emergency medical services if necessary
- Notify other designated camp authorities
- Document responses and complete incident reports

NARCOTIC ABUSE

Indicators can include:

- Red / bloodshot eyes, visual distortion
- Markedly dilated or constricted pupils
- Unexplained, repeated vomiting or abdominal pains
- Indistinct speech
- Excessive perspiration
- Delayed reflex action and lack of coordination
- Disorientation, dizziness, trembling hands
- Regular nosebleeds
- Injection marks / bruising / scabs / sores on arms, legs or private parts

Staff actions

- Notify the camp director, providing as much detail as possible
- If the person or persons suspected of abuse are a danger to the group in any way remove all learners from the immediate vicinity

Director / response team actions

- Get information from the staff and observe behaviour if needed.
- Activate the campsite emergency response team and brief them on the situation
- Isolate the individuals and verify the behaviour of individuals by:
  Talking to them and looking for signs mentioned above
  Getting information about the possible causes of behaviour
  Do a random drug test / breathalyser test on individuals if need be
- Address individual/s (if no abuse is indicated after interaction/testing) that their behaviour is of concern
- If abuse is evident, remove individuals from the group immediately
- Confront the individual/s and get as much information from them as possible
- Call/involve teachers and/or the principle in the matter and explain the procedures that led up to and followed the incident
- Call the police and emergency medical services if needed
- Call the family/parents explaining the situation and the procedures followed
- Protect the privacy of the family and the school by neither giving nor confirming information to the media or others without consent

- Remove individuals from the premises either by police escort or by means of school arrangement
- Notify educators/guides
- If deemed necessary by the director, call a staff meeting at the end of the day/camp to circulate additional information
- Complete appropriate incident reports and documentation

Juncture 4: Recovery

RECOVERY is the process of assisting people in dealing with the physical, psychological and emotional trauma associated with experiencing tragic events.

Recovery involves the implementation of a plan to return the activities of the camp to a normal learning environment as soon as possible.

Staff and clients need to be debriefed after an incident occurred. It is management's responsibility to determine who needs to be debriefed and to ensure that they are informed of the situation, the cause, how it was dealt with and what measures are being taken to resolve the occurrence. The purpose of debriefing is to get all related parties on the same page regarding the situation and the way forward, not to cause further trauma. Should counselling be needed as part of debriefing it is best to bring in a professional as soon as possible to help mediate the situation.

Data security

Your company needs to have extensive measures in place to protect your data and information. Cybercriminals are increasingly attacking companies by hacking their information or the information of their clients and then asking a ransom to return the information.

Back up your data and database on a secure online server as well as on an external storage device.

Ensure your administration computer is also password-protected.

No client information should be stored in the public domain and all measures should be taken to ensure this information is secure. There are companies and service providers that offer security software, including regular updates.

Marketing

Marketing can be either direct or indirect. Direct marketing delivers a message directly to a specific audience. Indirect marketing creates brand awareness by using channels where there are no direct communication with your audience.

Direct marketing mediums

Flyers – Flyers can be a very effective means of reaching a specific audience. They generally consist of eye-catching design features and strategically chosen words. It is also a relatively cheap medium that can be mass produced. The drawback of flyers is that they are generally regarded as spam. Flyers dropped in a mailbox or handed out at an intersection are generally trashed within seconds. It is thus vitally important that you make an impact and spark interest in your potential audience members at first glance of your flyer.

Note: Please consider the environmental impact of the waste created by printed media.

Newsletter – Newsletters can take several forms. Some companies print newsletters then mail or hand them out to clients. Others send electronic newsletters via email or email marketing software (EMS) such as MailChimp. They generally follow a format to provide necessary and interesting company news or information. It can be issued weekly, monthly, bi-monthly, quarterly, etc.

In order to capture and retain attention, newsletters need to be interesting. It is a very valuable tool for sharing information periodically.

Social media – Social media is the fastest growing marketing tool. There are numerous platforms you can use to market your company. It is instant and usually allows the sharing of both text and imagery. Using more than one platform is recommended as people favour different.
It is easy to link your social media platforms if you want to simultaneously post content to multiple ones.

It is important to use social media professionally and to remain conscious of what you place on your company's social media platforms.

Business cards – While not everyone needs them, business cards still hold value and make it easy for you to share your contact details with potential clients. Designers keep coming up with incredibly creative business cards using different materials and some even have a dual purpose, for example, paper containing seeds or a memory stick engraved with details.

Only print small batches to avoid waste when people resign or get promoted. Another solution is printing cards that only feature the company's details, instead of individualised business cards.

Text messaging – Bulk text messaging software and cheap tariffs have made this medium affordable. Messaging software allows you to personalise the message for each recipient while only using one template. You can also schedule messages to be sent on specific dates or at specific times. Messages can be automatically repeated and instant replies can be set up. This is a valuable tool that facilitates communication between parents and a campsite as information can reach hundreds of directly targeted members in an instant.

Promotional items or gift bags – While costly, these can be very effective when you apply a direct marketing strategy. If you want to target specific teachers at a school to promote a campsite or win over the school receptionist, use holidays or observances such as national teachers day or secretary day to treat those targeted key members at a school. Or take advantage of International Pancake Day to deliver pancakes to their classes with a message or information pack of your campsite.

After a few days, you can follow up with an email that encourages them to ask for any advice if they are planning a camp or if they need any more information on your campsite/centre and the services you provide.

Why should you try to win over receptionists? They are often the individuals who open and pass on your emails and newsletters to the decision makers. With their help, you have a better chance of reaching your target audience. Plus, liaising with a friendly person can only be beneficial.

Indirect marketing mediums

Publicity – Publicity is coverage in a news source that you generally do not pay for. Examples include an article in a newspaper or a magazine and a story on the radio or television. News sources need feel-good stories to fill space or time slots so send your stories or pictures to them.
Some sources will offer editorial space if you advertise with them.
Here are some examples of projects at an entrance, just off the main road. These features were erected to draw attention to the entrance and created instant publicity.

Windmill painted in support of breast cancer.

Minion and Angry Birds characters built from hay bales.

These road features also attract interest from road users. Some people pose with them and then post pictures on their social media and sends them to friends. It is therefore important that you always feature your company name or website nearby or in the picture frame.

Souvenirs – A souvenir can be a powerful marketing tool. You can sell items with your company name and logo on them in your tuck shop or at your office that clients can take home. Other people will see your name and talk to your clients about you. Word of mouth is very powerful. Items could include, button badges, sunglasses, caps, hats, scarves, t-shirts, cups, bottles, pens, pencils, etc.

Social media – Social media can also be an indirect marketing tool. A page or platform where you post photos of camps and groups can attract parents and friends who will see your brand and projects. Make sure you have permission to use pictures or videos (see page 11).

Brand consistency – Consistent brand name and logo use across all media are very important. Using the same colours, fonts and shapes have physiological benefits as it helps build trust through recognition. It is your brand identity. For example, if a specific tree in a specific colour is used with a brand name in a specific font it will later be associated with the brand/company. Eventually, people may come to recognise the specific tree or brand name without one or the other element.
Add your name and logo to every form of communication you use, including signage around the centre/camp. Even brand your menus and programmes.

Clothing – Branded clothing and uniforms help your clients or potential clients to identify your staff. Add your website on the back of clothing so it is easier to see and visit. Photos of staff wearing branded clothing can also lead to website visits without any effort.

Car branding – Putting your logo, company name and website on your company vehicles is a cheap way to reach a large number of people in a variety of places. People sitting in traffic or passing your parked car can visit your website and reach you in that manner.
IMPORTANT: A branded car puts you in the public eye which means irresponsible, aggressive or dangerous driving can hurt your brand.

Signage – Having proper signage not only makes it easier for your clients to find your business but also serves as a marketing tool. Ensure your signage is visible, readable and clear from a distance. Replace old, sun-faded signs timeously.

You can ask suppliers to sponsor your signage. Many soft drink or ice cream suppliers have a budget to erect signage for their clients that then features the brands of both parties.

Searchability – An online presence is a must in this day and age. You need to have a website or page clients can refer to. When people search words related to your industry you want your name and website to appear on the first page of the search results.

There are many companies that you can pay to boost your visibility, but you can also improve it yourself. Here are a few tips and tricks you can try:

- Make sure there are NO spelling mistakes on your website.
- Regular website updates will count in your favour.
- You can link your social media accounts to your website so that every time you post something it is fed to your webpage. This will count as an "update of information".
- Make use of the many free advertising platforms for promoting your services. Every place on the web that mentions your company name counts as a citation for a search engine.
- Visit your website from as many different computers as you can. This creates traffic which leads to search engines noticing you. I have heard of people who use demo phones and computers in shops to search for their websites and then leave the page open on the devices. Not only does this create traffic but it opens a longer session with your site which will improve your ranking and the next user of that device will also see your webpage when they look at the phone or laptop. This is an extreme case but nonetheless an example of the lengths one can go to in order to improve your ranking.
- Make sure your details (especially your address and phone number) are correct on search engines as well as on navigational platforms and maps.
- Make use of website analytical tools to track the behaviours of those who visit your website. Knowing where clients click or tend to go can be used to your advantage as you can start placing the most important information on the relevant pages and areas.

QR codes – Create a few QR codes using free online software that directs people to your website. These QR codes can then be printed on stickers that you can place on your company vehicles and equipment. People, especially children, love using technology and scanning these codes to see where they lead to.

Commemorative books – Clients loves to sit and page through booklets showing the history of your site or camp. It is a good reading resource you can have in your accommodation, seating areas and office waiting area.

It is also a fantastic tool to see how you have grown over the years. Make a habit of it to regularly document the happenings of your company and include items such as newsletters and flyers to build up a little archive of happenings.

Notes on marketing to schools

When you want to market your campsite or centre to a school, it is ideal to visit them in person.

Teachers and principals want to see you in order to ask you questions about your company and the programmes you offer. Be prepared and take business cards, flyers and newsletters with you so that you can leave something behind.

Do schedule appointments and keep your appointments. Do not just rock up at a school and expect to meet with a teacher or the principal.

Study the school's website and social media pages beforehand to make small talk or to congratulate the school on achievements.

Ensure you have all the information on your campsite such as tariffs, availability, etc. at hand.

Make every client feel special and make the booking and deciding on a campsite process just as enjoyable as the camp itself. If clients struggle to get information from you or feel unimportant, they can easily go to another site or centre.

CHAPTER 2
POLICIES AND PROCEDURES

Why do we have policies? Sometimes an event, a string of events, the occurrence of an incident or a complain leads to a policy or rule to be set — sometimes camp managers or governing boards set policies as guidelines to staff.

What policies are needed? There is no way one can have an all-inclusive set of policies that will work for the centre or campsite. There is, however, a few policies that are universal, below will follow a few policies that one can tailor to suit the needs of your organisation and others can be added to your set as the need arises.

Tattoos

People get tattoos for many reasons and the trend is bound to stay.

Reasons include remembering a person or an event, self-expression, artistic freedom, reminders of spiritual or religious/cultural traditions, identification with a group, etc.

This makes it very difficult to set a policy on tattoos. I have encountered several versions of policies over the years, from banning tattoos as a whole, to allow tattoos under clothing (and everything in between). One particular policy I tend to agree with is that tattoos are allowed, but they should not offend anyone in any way and should be covered as far as possible.

Piercings

Ear piercings, body piercings (for example arm or navel piercings) and face piercings (for example eyebrow or lip piercings) can get caught on equipment or natural elements and pose a safety risk to the guide and potentially the client.

Professionalism and piercings: Some sites have a professional appearance policy that limits the number of visible piercings a person may have.

Hair policies

As with piercings, hair is sometimes dealt with in a professional appearance policy with regards to colour, length and styles.

Long, loose hair or hair covering one or both eyes pose a safety risk in the camping industry as hair can get caught in equipment and impair vision during activities. The same holds true for loose hair bands or ribbons.

Pregnancy

Staff and clients who are pregnant need medical clearance before they are allowed to participate in activities/exercise. Generally, campsites have staff policies in place but they should also have policies that address clients in their 3rd trimester of pregnancy who want to camp.

Sexual orientation and gender identity

All humans deserve to be respected and accepted. We need to ensure that our facilities are developed in such a way as to encourage acceptance of all gender identities and discourage offensive behaviour or discrimination in any form. This philosophy applies to everyone – clients, staff and beyond.

LGBTQIA is an umbrella term that stands for Lesbian, Gay, Bisexual, Transgender, Queer, Intersex and Asexual. The LGBTQIA glossary continues to change, evolve and grow.

Clothing policies

Though many campsites and centres have uniforms, clothing policies are very important, especially with regards to swimwear. Women's bikinis, men's swimming briefs and white or revealing swimwear are not allowed. Short shorts, tight pants, miniskirts and revealing clothing such as spaghetti strap tops and sleeveless shirts do not belong in a professional working environment.

Relationships

Personal relationships between staff and clients/children are not allowed, under any circumstances. At many sites, personal relationships between staff members are not allowed either. This includes sexual interactions of any kind.

Some sites also have a policy that prevents younger staff from dating someone schoolgoing children.

Another area of concern is staff making contact with clients/children via digital platforms and electronic devices, whether it is accepting friendship requests or sending text messages. VERY strict policies need to be in place and this type of interaction or exchange of contact details is generally not allowed.

Professional relationship and interaction

Staff and clients/children sharing tents, rooms and ablutions are also troublesome and may cause problems. Same-sex sharing, in general, is acceptable but strict rules and policies should be in place to regulate conduct, for example, staff members are not permitted to change or shower in front of clients/children.

Many camps have open-plan shower facilities where same-sex students shower together. These facilities need to be updated.

Tip: How can privacy be increased in bathrooms?

Existing shower doors can be sandblasted or covered in a frosted film if they are transparent. Shower cubicles, featuring two units covered by a curtain or door for privacy, can be designed: A wet area for showering and a dry area for undressing and dressing.

Screens can be placed between urinals for privacy.

Drugs and alcohol

Most campsites have a very strict (often zero-tolerance) drug and alcohol or substance abuse policy that applies to staff and clients. Normally a blood alcohol level of 0.000 needs to be maintained when working with children.

Rules and laws on multidrug or alcohol testing on employees differ around the globe and management needs to adhere to local law requirements.

The Occupational Health and Safety Act of South Africa Regulation 2A states that every employer has a duty to stop persons from entering or remaining at work if they appear to be under the influence of alcohol or drugs.

However, you must have a substance abuse policy in place in which you describe the need for multidrug and alcohol testing as well as how testing will be implemented. Examples would be random drug tests or post-accident testing, etc.

If a company wants to start testing and has not done so in the past, it is required to give its employees notice of its intention to start testing (normally one or two months in advance).

Can an employee refuse to take a test?

Yes, you cannot force someone to take a drug or alcohol test. However, your substance abuse policy can state that refusal to test will be seen as an admission of guilt and will result in disciplinary steps against such an employee.

Multidrug saliva tests are more hygienic and less invasive than multidrug urine tests.

Smoking

Create a dedicated safe smoking area. Staff should be prohibited from smoking near clients/children and from smoking where they can be seen by clients/children. Most camps also ban smoking within five metres of buildings and vehicles.

Criminal records

Potential campsite/centre employees should submit a valid police clearance certificate along with their other application documents whether they will be working with children directly (group leader) or indirectly (administrator, gardener, etc.).

South Africa has a National Register for Sex Offenders (NRSO). It contains the names of those found guilty of sexual offences against children or people who are intellectually disabled.

The Criminal Law (Sexual Offences and Related Matters) Amendment Act, 2007 (Act No. 32 of 2007) requires all organisations working with children and intellectually disabled persons to prevent those listed on the NRSO from working with children or a person who is mentally disabled.

Employers need to check that the names of employees and potential employees are not on the list. If an employee is listed, employment should be terminated immediately.

This contents of the NRSO is not open to the public, but names and identity numbers can be checked with agencies or attorneys, along with polygraph tests and a police clearance certificate.

Drinking water policy

If you have taps on your campsite or premises that supply water that is not of drinking quality (greywater, water from a dam or rainwater collector), you can paint the tap red and put a tap lock on.

Taps supplying safe drinking water can be painted blue. Remember to explain it to visitors either verbally or via signs.

Swimming pool policy

If you have a pool or pools on site, chances are good you have a set of swimming pool rules in place already. It is, however, a good idea to have a policy in place as well. Swimming pools should be enclosed and locked at all times. Swimming after dark and glass items near the pool are usually prohibited.

Sponsors

The camping industry always welcomes sponsorship. It is the responsibility of managers and staff to ensure that the sponsors get the acknowledgement they deserve. For example, mention sponsors and use their logos on menus, programmes and other printed materials; Displaying items (products, flags, brochures, etc.) is another great way to honour sponsors.

Though sponsorship might always be welcome, make sure there is sponsor-brand alignment in terms of values and mission. For example, if you have a zero-tolerance policy against drinking, you should not accept sponsorship from a brewery.

CHAPTER 3
SAVING RESOURCES AND SELF-HELP

Snake handling equipment

Keeping a campsite completely snake-free is impossible. Most campsites correctly catch and then release snakes where they will be safe and well away from any domestic or commercial properties. Some, however, kill all snakes they come across. (Note: Many people are bitten because they try to kill snakes.) Whatever your method or motivation, dealing with snakes requires equipment.

Snake education is vital, as you have to identify snakes before attempting to handle them. Some snakes require speciality snake handling tools while others are harmless and actually beneficial to have around.

Before approaching a snake that can spit, for example, you need specific safety equipment such as eye protection.

If you cannot identify the snake for whatever reason, use the same equipment as you would for a spitting snake.

Protect your eyes and mouth (ideally with a full face visor) and wear hard leather boots as a precaution.

Familiarise yourself with a snake hook before you actually have to use it. Staff members also need to undergo snake handling training. Snake hooks can be used to lift rocks, logs and other hiding places.

Some snakes, for example, puff adders, should not be handled with a short hook as they can instantly strike in any direction.

Never underestimate a snake's strength.

Snake tongs can be effective, but they need to be used with care. Because you cannot gauge the pressure, you could end up injuring the snake.

The size of a snake storage tube or tub matters. You should be able to safely insert and release the snake without endangering yourself or harming the snake.

Snake-handling equipment is easy and cheap to make and can work just as well as the equipment you can purchase.

Snake hook

If you have an old golf club and a piece of aluminium rod it is easy to make a snake hook.

First, remove the club from its handle. Next, bend the rod into a hook shape. Then, use epoxy glue to attach the hook to the club handle.

Snake tubes

Material: 110 mm perforated drainage pipe (used for underground drainage). Length: 1 metre.

Glue a stop fitting on the one end and a screw fitting on the other (see picture on the previous page).

Leave the parts to set for 4 hours before use so that all the fumes from the PVC glue can evaporate.

To seek shelter, most snakes will enter a tube placed in front of them, which makes catching the snake very easy.

WARNING: A snake will always turn around to face the entrance of the pipe to protect itself, so never pick up the open end of the pipe with your bare hands.

If a snake needs to be stored for release at a later stage, place the tube in a dark place far away from pets and chemicals where it cannot be affected by direct sunlight or another heat source.

To release the snake, unscrew the cap while keeping your hands as far away from the open end of the pipe as possible. With the open end away from you, gently shake the tube, allowing the snake to slide out and onto the ground.

Tips on water saving

Toilets

Toilet cisterns can use as much as 21 litres of water per flush. Newer, slimmer toilet cisterns use about 9 litres of water per flush. To save water, you can fill old 500 ml plastic bottles with rocks, sand or water before sealing and placing them inside your toilets' cisterns. Two 500 ml plastic bottles placed in one cistern will displace 1 litre of water every time the cistern fills up, saving you 1 litre of water per flush.

Note: Some toilet systems need a certain amount of water to flush properly. Displacing too much water might prevent this. Also, ensure that the bottles do not interfere with or become stuck in the cistern's flushing or filling mechanisms.

Water-saving showerheads

You can easily save hundreds of litres of water per day just by changing showerheads

One shower tested at a camp had a 30 litres per minute flow rate. It was replaced with a showerhead that expels 9 litres per minute which instantly saves 21 litres of water per minute, without reducing the quality of the shower.

In a campsite bathroom with 10 showers, you will save 210 litres of water per minute.

When shopping for showerheads, look at the per minute flow rate.

Another option is flow control valves that can be applied to showerheads and taps.

Tap aerators

Tap aerators can be screwed onto existing taps. They add bubbles and in a sense increases water volume. In the kitchen or scullery, bubbles also help loosen food on plates. Aerators can reduce the flow of water by as much as 50% while facilitating adequate pressure.

Gardens

To conserve water, plant indigenous plants and ones that do not need much water, for example, succulents. There are many beautiful species to choose from.

Irrigation

Irrigating during the hottest time of the day is ineffective and wastes water through rapid evaporation. Rather set sprinklers to water at night or early morning when it is cooler. Irrigating in windy conditions is not advised as the water blows away. Consider a drip irrigation system which enables targeted, controlled watering.

Leaks

It is estimated that we lose approximately 40% of clean water through leaks in pipelines that can easily be fixed. Go around your campsites and make a list of leaking toilets, pipes, taps and tanks. Report the leaks to your maintenance team as soon as possible.

Pipe isolation

Hot water pipes should be isolated. Pipes that are above ground or exposed are easy to cover with pipeline isolation. Cost-effective alternatives are fabric, newspaper and scrap paper.

Here is an example of pipes wrapped in wet scrap paper (5 – 10 mm) painted with glue and covered with a split PVC pipe to protect from the elements.

The same can be done with cold water pipes to prevent overheating in summer and freezing and bursting in winter.

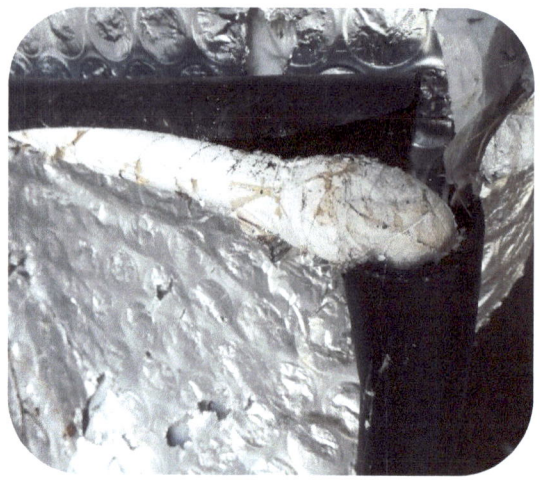

Tips for energy saving

Motion sensor lights

You can save electricity (and money) by fitting motion sensor lights in rooms that are frequently entered for short periods, such as storerooms, pantries and walk-in fridges. They will switch on when motion is detected and automatically switch off after a short while or when motion is no longer detected. This solution is cost-effective and easy to execute.

Geyser blankets

These blankets help keep the heat in and the cold out by adding an additional layer of insulation. They are very easy to install and very effective. Geyser blankets are made from a reflective foil that resembles bubble wrap and covers entire water heaters.

Geyser timers

A controversial topic. Some maintain a geyser that is left on uses less power than one that is repeatedly switched on and off, as it has to reheat water that has cooled down each time. A geyser that is properly isolated is more energy efficient since the water does not completely cool down when switched off. Unfortunately, this is not a viable option if you need hot water 24/7. In a cottage or staff room where hot water is only needed in the mornings and evenings, an isolated geyser is a fantastic power safer. You can set the timer to switch the geyser on 30 minutes before hot water is needed and switch it off after. This way, power will only be consumed for a short time.

Solar geyser

Solar technology has been around for a long time and is becoming more efficient. Still, it may not be ideal for campsites that can facilitate really large groups or regions with a cloudy, rainy climate Hybrid options are available that allow you to switch from solar to electrical when needed. You may also want to try the following:

- To heat more water, you can connect a larger holding tank (fitted with an electrical heating element) to solar tubes with a circulation pump. A 12-volt system, connected to a solar panel, can power the circulation pump so that it only circulates the water to the solar heating tubes when the sun shines.
- Connect your hot water outlet on the solar geyser to the cold-water inlet on your electrical geyser. This way hot water from your electric geyser is replaced with preheated water from the solar geyser that needs little or no heating. The result: Increased hot water capacity and power saving.

Upcycling around the centre

Give used items a new purpose at your campsite or centre.

Here are a few ideas:

Tyre chairs

Children can significantly reduce the lifespan of regular outdoor chairs. A tyre chair, on the other hand, can be rolled, thrown, jumped on and rocked and still stay intact.

Drill holes in the sidewall of an old tyre and use nylon rope to weave a grid. Tyres can be stacked and fastened with bolts to create height. If you want to construct several tyre chairs, draw up a drilling guideline on a piece of paper or plywood for the different tyre sizes to guide your drilling so your weave pattern stays square.

Tyre dog house

Turn two tyres inside out and mount them back to back to form a cosy and dry den for your campsite guard dogs.

Soccer goal posts

Use PVC pipe and fittings to easily construct these cheap soccer goal posts.

Saving resources

Saving in the kitchen

Proper planning and a few simple practices followed by all staff can result in significant savings.

Bread

Do not order loaves with high tops. Their slices do not always fit into toasters and double toasting increases electricity use., Instead, ask your baker for sandwich bread loaves with flat tops.

Leftover food

Leftover food can be used in upcoming meals so plan your menus accordingly.

For example, use leftover scrambled eggs from breakfast for macaroni and cheese served in the evening, as the recipe requires scrambled egg anyway. French toast or leftover bread can be used in bread pudding.

Leftover toast can be processed into crumbs and used to thicken stews or coat fried chicken.

Breakfast porridge such as oatmeal can be frozen and re-boiled at a later stage before serving.

Remember: Leftover food should be cooled down as quickly as possible and then frozen or stored in airtight containers or bags. Once defrosted, you should never refreeze it.

Cold chain

Maintaining the cold chain of fresh and frozen produce is vital. Suppliers ensure that products are transported and stored at the optimal temperatures. It is the responsibility of the purchaser to ensure that products such as dairy, meat, fresh/frozen vegetables and fruit are kept and transported at optimal temperatures. Food that gets a thermal shock from being exposed to heat (direct sunlight, temperatures in a hot car, etc.) for just a few minutes will suffer from a reduced shelf life.

Paintball tip

Refilling paintball canisters that are not empty can be wasteful or dangerous. You either need to release (and waste) all the air before refilling or guess the amount of gas you need to replace. The latter is unsafe and can be costly when the safety valves blow off and need replacement. To prevent this, you can use a stencil to paint the canister's empty weight on it. The next time you need to refill, you will know the start weight and can then safely refill canisters that are not completely empty.

Fire hydrants lockable cases

Children tend to find fire extinguishers irresistible. To prevent mischief or damage, place your extinguishers in cabinets with breakable glass for key access. This mostly stops children from messing around with the extinguisher.

CHAPTER 4
BASICS ON MAINTENANCE

Trailer sockets

Rewiring a trailer's connection socket is a maintenance task that people very often procrastinate on, usually because they need to first figure out where all those coloured wires go. This one time, I arrived at a campsite where they were rewiring the car's connection coupling to fit that of a trailer, not knowing there is a standard factory connection.

There are flat pin connectors and round pin connectors, both in 6-pin, 7-pin, 9-pin and 13-pin variations. The most commonly used variation in South Africa, which vehicles are factory issued with, is the round 7-pin connector.

Here is a picture of a factory standard 7-pin connection on a vehicle.

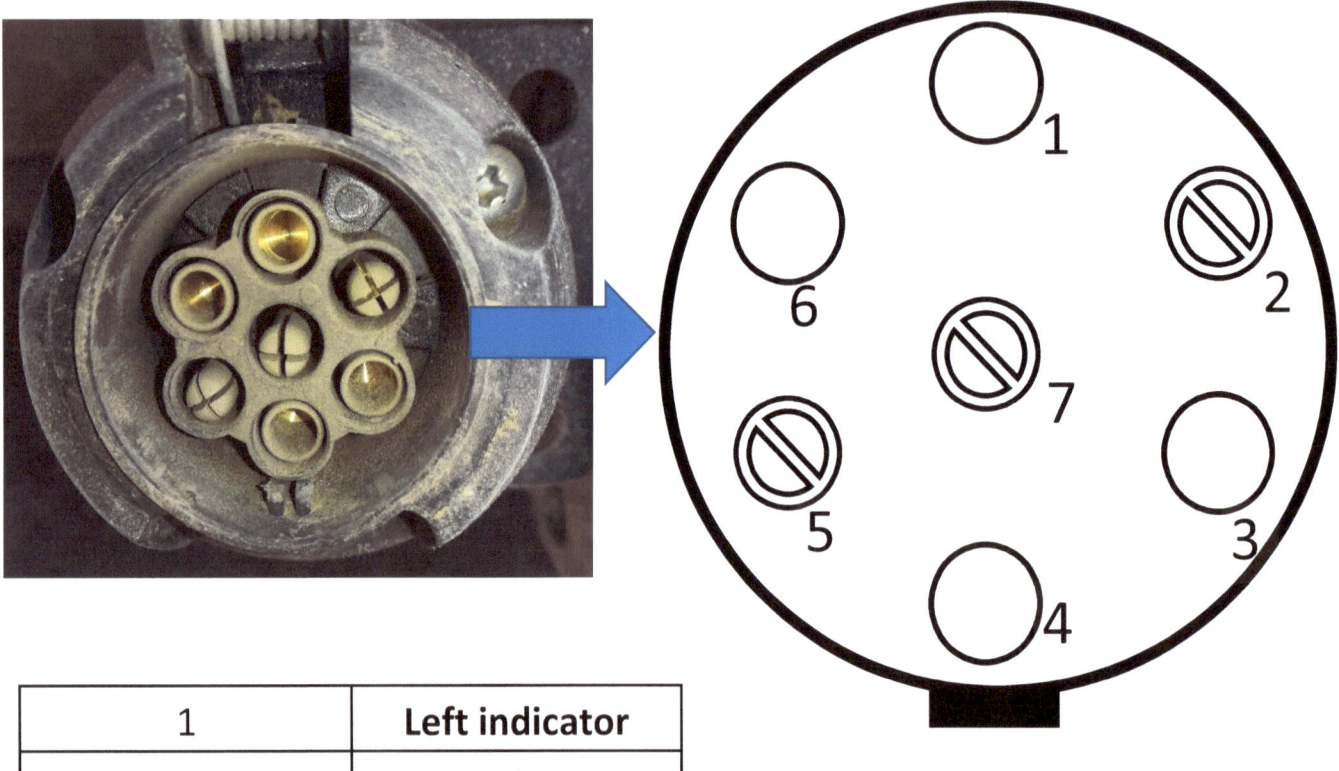

1	Left indicator
2	Auxiliary
3	Earth
4	Right indicator
5	R/H lights
6	Brake lights
7	L/H lights

The trailer's plug looks like this:

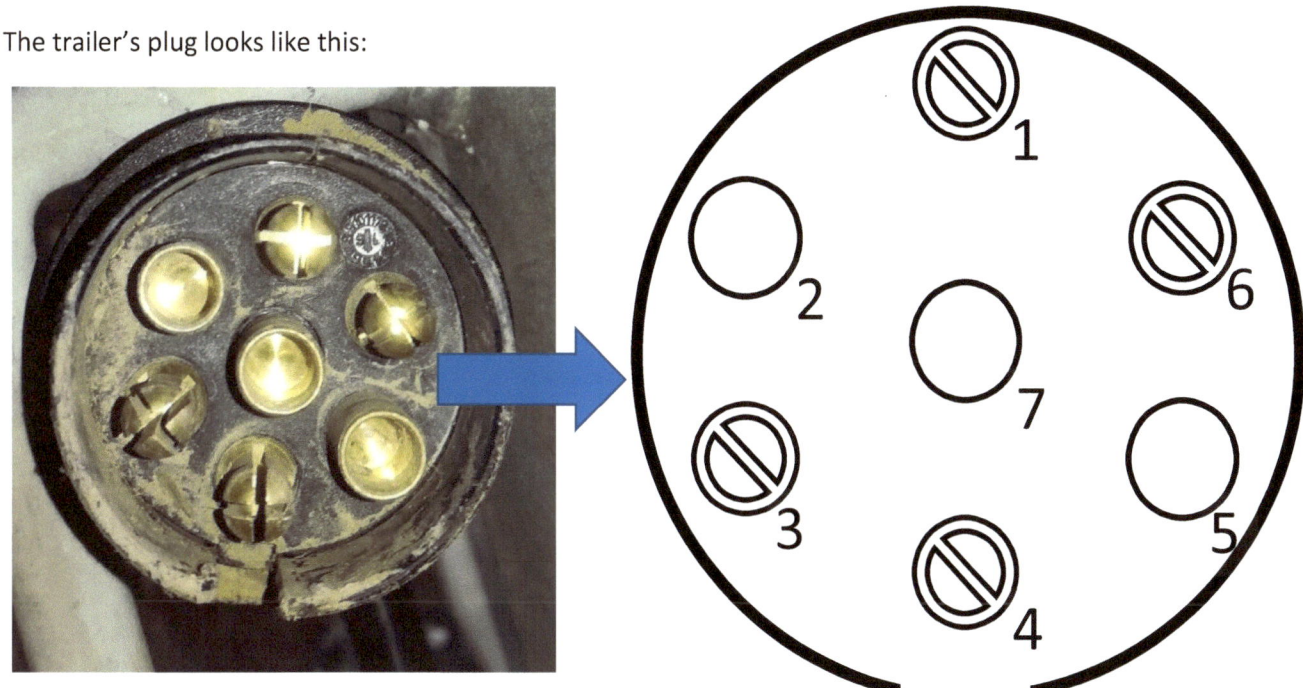

Always keep a connector chart handy, like the one provided below, for each trailer. Write down each function's corresponding colour then clearly mark the printout and store it with the vehicle registration papers. This will save you hours when a trailer plug needs to be replaced.

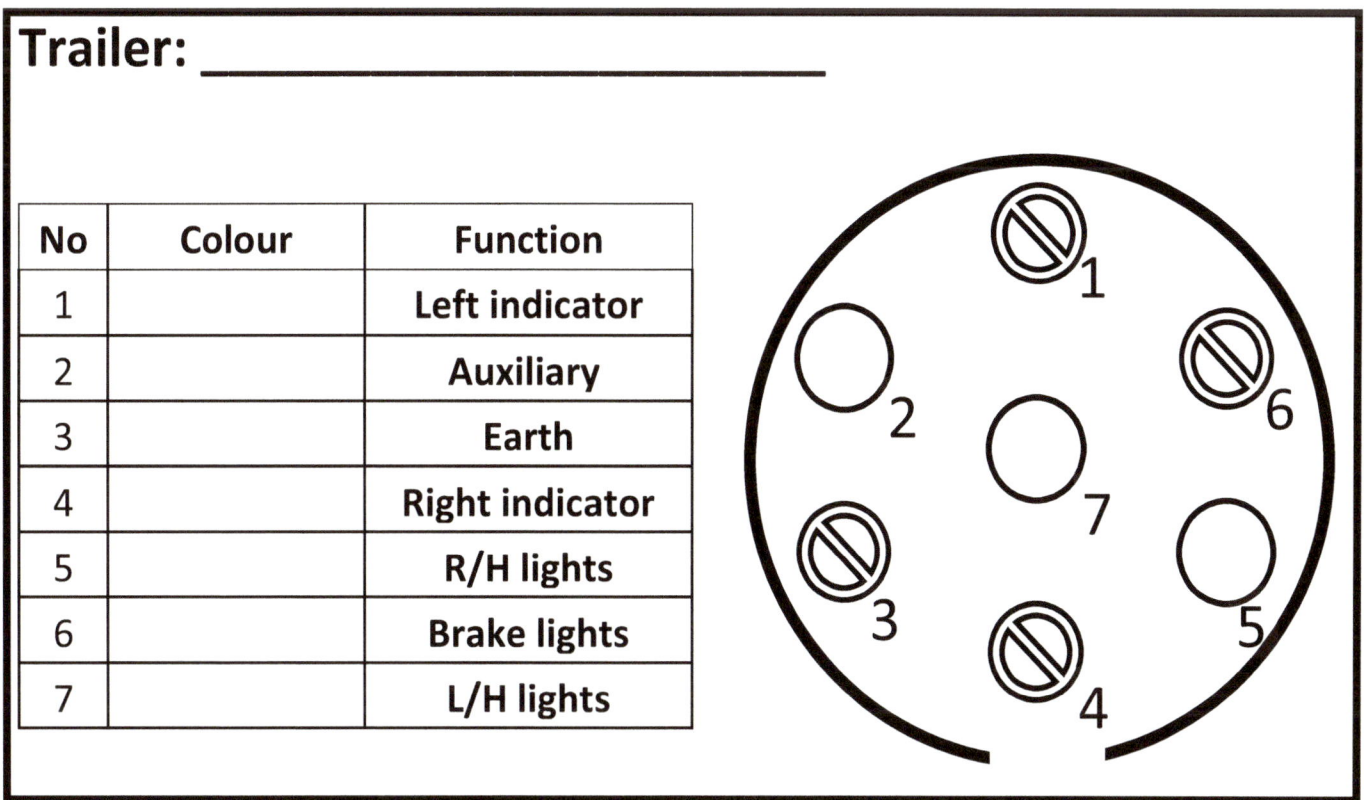

Trailer: _____

No	Colour	Function
1		Left indicator
2		Auxiliary
3		Earth
4		Right indicator
5		R/H lights
6		Brake lights
7		L/H lights

Electrical plugs

Sometimes a basic task, for example connecting a plug to an appliance, can be a nuisance if you forget the basics.

Remember: When you cut the cord of a new appliance, you lose your warranty.

Safety first: Switch off and unplug the appliance from all power sources (this includes back up batteries).

In South Africa, we use 220v power and our outlets have three prongs.

Look at the flat side of a plug, held upright, with the back plate removed.

The earth wire (normally green and yellow, or sometimes bare copper) leads into the large top prong.

The live wire (normally red or brown) leads into the right prong.

The neutral wire (normally blue or black) leads into the left prong.

If an appliance does not have an earth wire, simply connect the live and neutral wires in their respective positions and leave the earth prong unwired.

Some appliances, mostly lights and lamps, only have two uncoloured wires. In this case, it does not matter which wire is connected to live and which to neutral and the earth prong remains unwired.

Three-phase Plugs

Please consult an electrician before connecting three-phase plugs. The process is complex and could result in serious damage to your appliances. Three-phase plugs have three live wires and one neutral wire (4 prongs). Some also have a prong for the earth (total 5 prongs). In some cases, when live wires have been switched, the motor of the appliance (for example a water pump) will run in the opposite direction and operate incorrectly.

Distribution boxes

Always close and lock electrical distribution boxes to keep water, animals and children out. You also have to have a High Voltage Sign directly above or on the distribution box.

Ensure that ALL your breakers and isolators are clearly marked.

Breaker VS Isolator = Breakers and isolators look very similar, but their functions differ greatly. A breaker is a trippable connector. When there is a problem on the connected line, the breaker will trip and cut the electrical supply to that connection. This protects your wires, appliance and electrical system. An Isolator, on the other hand, is a connector you can only manually switch on or off. It will not trip automatically.

It is good practice to label your electrical outlets and light switches to indicate their power sources. This allows one to switch off a specific breaker when there is a fault on the switch or socket and helps to quickly identify a problem. The power outlet shown in the photo is marked DB7B5. This wall socket, therefore, gets its power from distribution board number 7 (DB7), breaker number 5 (B5).

Recommended: Place your emergency contact details and an electrical plan of the premises inside or next to the distribution box.

NB: The electrical input side of a breaker and isolator is on the top and the power output is on the bottom. If breakers and isolators are wired incorrectly, they may not function properly.

When you have a three-phase earth leakage and you distribute to single-phase breakers, it is important to spread the load amongst the three phases. Do not connect all lights and plugs to just one phase. Your electrician will distribute the load and check that your distribution boxes are correctly wired.

Ask your electrician to not connect the light in the room where your distribution box sits to your earth leakage. This way, if the power trips, you will still be able to see your distribution box.

Geyser and solar geyser explained

Ensuring clients have hot water is crucial in the camping and hospitality industries. Solar geysers seldom meet the needs of a campsite that accommodates many children. However, with the correct installation, a solar geyser can reduce power consumption significantly.

Refer to solar geyser connection options explained on page 58.

There are far more effective ways to heat water, for example with heat pumps, but the initial investment discourages campsites from installing them.

You can build your own solar water heater with these items in your workshop:

Curved fittings and black PVC pipe.

Cut black PVC pipe in lengths and connect the ends with curved fittings to form a U-shape at both ends that will allow the water to flow from one pipe into the next until you have a grid of pipes that can heat water by laying in the sun.

One also gets U-bends for commercial use. They can save time when it comes to connecting pipes and make it easier to create an even grid.

Secure the grid in an area where it will have high exposure to direct sunlight, for example, on a roof. It is important to have a low-flow system so that the water has time to heat in the grid's pipes.

This is a great way to heat swimming pools in a cost-effective way.

How to reverse a door lock

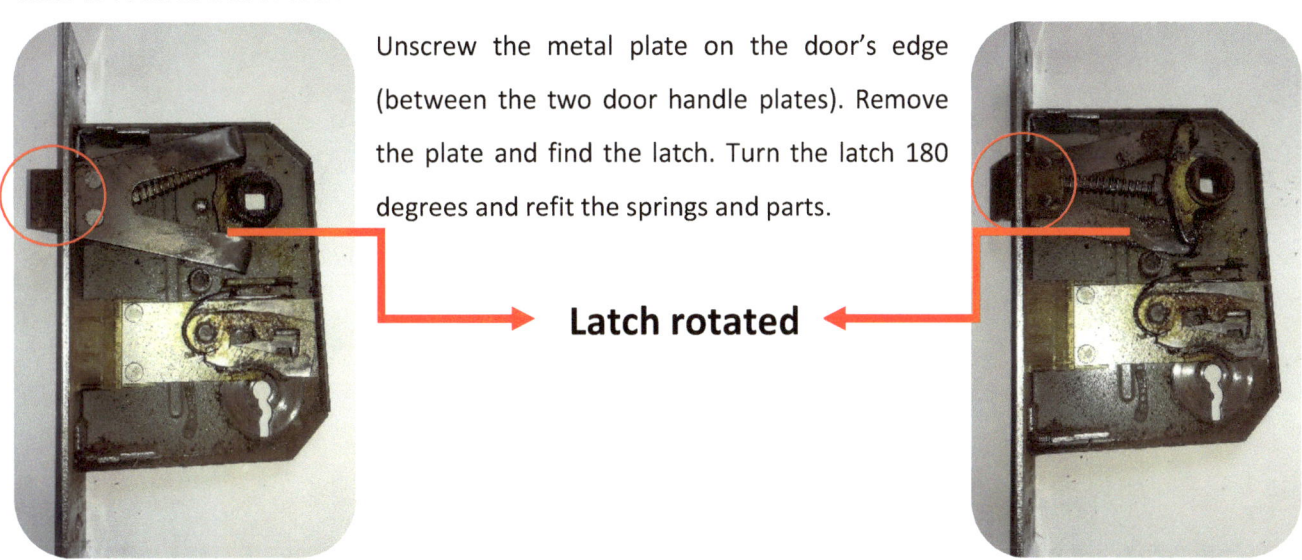

Unscrew the metal plate on the door's edge (between the two door handle plates). Remove the plate and find the latch. Turn the latch 180 degrees and refit the springs and parts.

Latch rotated

Basic toolbox

For basic maintenance purposes, a toolbox should at least contain the following:

Pliers	Screwdriver set	Drill with bits
Long nose pliers	Measurer	Pipe cutter
Side cutters	Spirit level	Combination square
Socket set with ratchet	Utility knife	Hot glue gun
Spanner set	Vice grip	Silicone tube gun
Claw hammer	Allen key set	<u>Consumables:</u>
Saw	Putty knife	Isolating tape
Pipe wrench	Chisel	Waterproofing tape
Adjustable wrench shifting	Staple gun	Cable ties

Tip: For stubborn bolts, put the correct size spanner over the bolt and hook another spanner to the front. This increases the leverage, making it easier to undo or tighten.

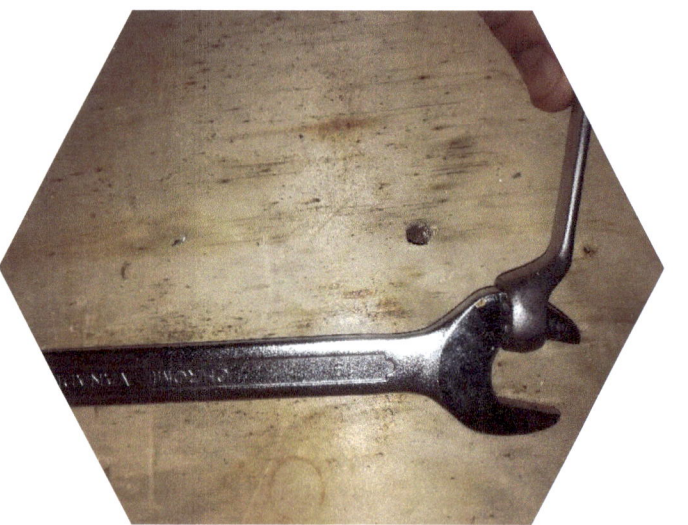

How to fix a burst copper water pipe

The golden rule that keeps water pipes from bursting in winter is pipe isolation (see page 57).

Copper pipes that are above ground or exposed are a lot easier to fix than concealed pipes. If you suspect a leak or burst in a pipe that is embedded in the wall you will have to chisel the plaster away to expose the pipe and leak.

Use a pipe cutter if there is space for it to fit around the pipe. Otherwise, use a metal saw then sand the edges with a fine file or sanding paper. Cut out the damaged piece of pipe and replace it with a connector to join the pipe. If the damage occurred over the length of the pipe, it may be necessary to use two connectors with a new piece of pipe in the middle.

Sealant tapes can temporarily fix leaks. A rubber tube wrapped around a leak, tightened with wire, is another temporary fix.

If you need to fix existing pipes, weld-on sockets can save you money, unless you have chlorine and lime in your water. The combination creates a residue that prevents the solder from attaching to the pipe.

PVC drain pipes

Fittings and PVC pipes can sometimes be glued together with PVC glue. For best results, use a piece of fine sanding paper to rough up the tip of the pipe and the inside of the fitting before applying PVC glue. This gives the glue grip.

Other fittings have rubber seals. It can be difficult to insert the pipe into this seal due to space limitations. Use a little bit of soapy water as a lubricant to slide the pipe into the fitting or spray oil/silicon lubricant on the seal and the pipe edge before you slide it in.

For best results, use a file to taper the edge of the pipe to avoid damage to the seal upon insertion.

How to fix a leaky tap

A leaky tap can generally be fixed by fitting it with a new seal.

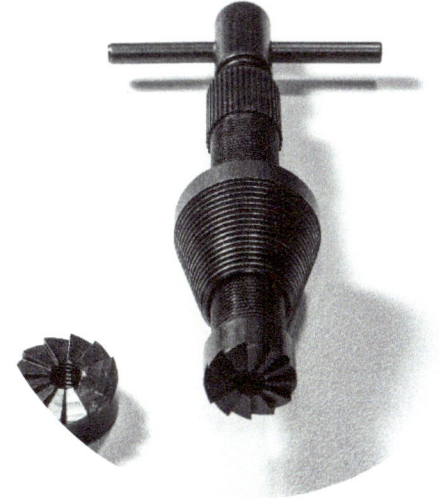

Before you start, turn off the water supply. Next, unscrew the cap underneath the handle (you may need to remove the handle). Underneath this cap, you can use a wrench or shifting spanner to unscrew the inner part of the tap where the washer or seal sits. Now you can replace the old seal with a new one. To remove lime build-up or residue inside the hold of the tap, use a cutter before putting the tap back together.

How to join a power cord

Remove a section of the insulation around the coloured wires. Be careful not to damage the protective (coloured) layers of the wires inside. Now strip back a section the coloured insulation on each of the wires to expose a centimetre of the strands within. Use a connector block to connect wires of the same colour with each other then cover the connection with isolation tape.

How to check for air or gas leaks

Here is a quick, easy and free way to check for leaks after installing any type of air or gas line: Mix some dishwashing detergent with water and use a soft brush to generously coat each connection and fitting. If there is a leak, bubbles will form upon application.

Cream painted class 1 copper pipes are typically installed for gas cooking systems. These pipes are expensive. As an alternative, buy a class 1 water copper pipe and paint it with cream enamel paint. Mercedes-Benz Cream is the closest match to the industrial pipe's colour

Remember: All pipes, fittings and taps must be SABS (South African Bureau of Standards) approved. Gas system taps/levers must have red or yellow handles/sleeves.

How to get a 45-degree angle

When you need to cut a piece of wood or iron at a 45-degree angle, but you do not have a compass or square in your toolbox, simply measure the width of the piece and mark this measurement on the side of the object. Now draw a line from the opposite corner to the measured mark. This will produce a 45-degree angle cut line.

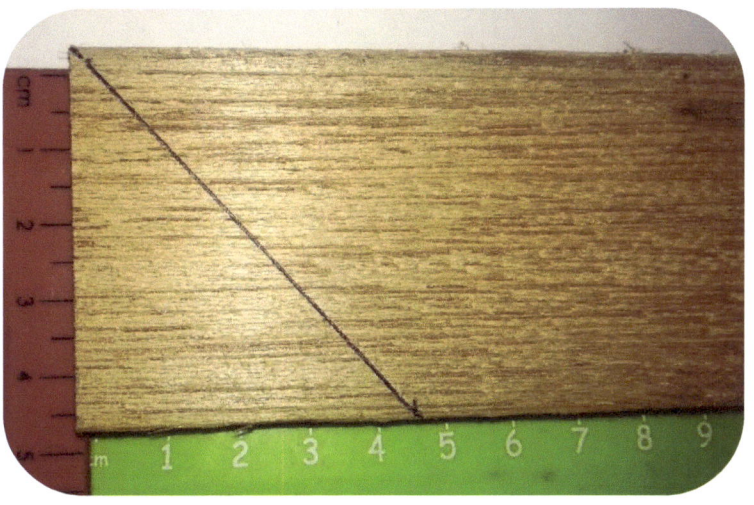

Septic tanks

Most campsites in South Africa are situated in remote locations and have no means of connecting to municipal sewage lines. These sites mainly run on septic tank systems. A septic tank is a very effective, small-scale sewage treatment plant.

The basic mechanics of a septic tank:

Sewage water is collected in a series of pipes that connect to the septic tank. Inside the septic tank, decomposers and bacteria break down the sewage. Solid flocculants sink to the bottom of the tank whilst scum floats to the surface. The "clean" water sits between these layers. This water is then channelled away to be treated or naturally filtered into a soakaway drain.

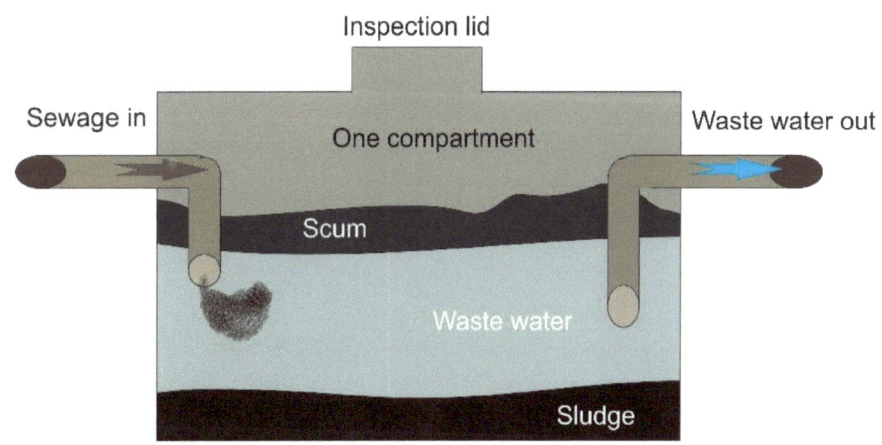

While a one-stage septic tank, like the one shown above, is widely used, it is preferable to use a multistage septic tank.

Here is an example of a multistage septic tank designed with mass use in mind.

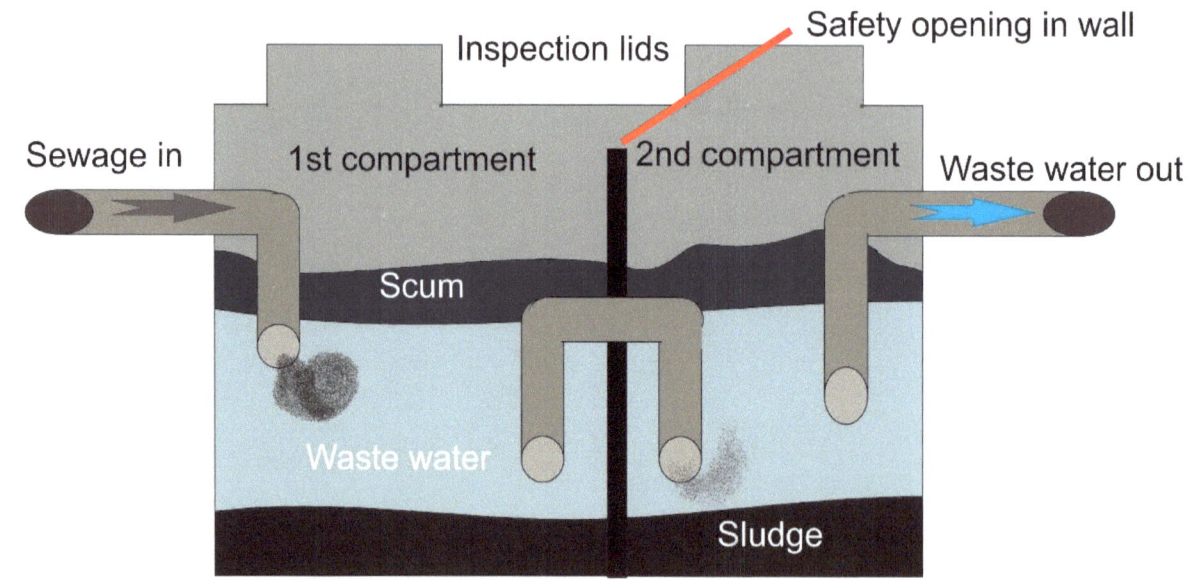

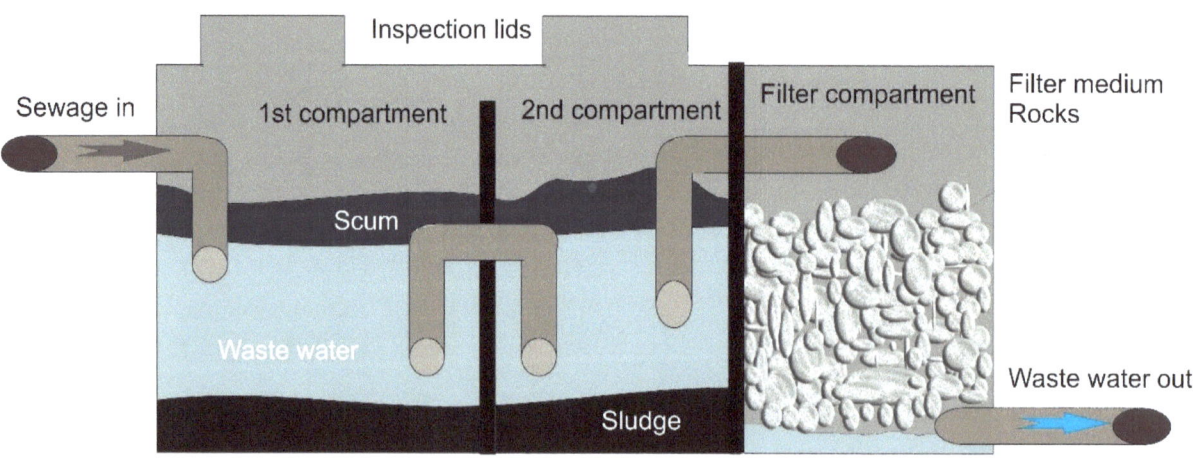

The raw sewage line connects to the first compartment of the tank. A bent inlet pipe connects the first compartment to the second compartment at about mid-height. The second tank's outlet reaches about the same depth as the bent inlet that connects compartment one and two. After entering the second compartment, bacteria can further break down the sewage and remaining particles in suspension. A third compartment can be constructed. This filter (also called French) drain provides a final filtering opportunity before water leaves the system. This filter compartment is usually filled with gravel or rock.

NB: Ensure that there is a safety opening between the first and second compartments. This way, if there is a blockage or if someone or something falls in, access and exiting is possible. The inlet pipe will sit below the opening to ensure the space is water free. Each tank's outlet <u>must</u> also be lower than the inlet to prevent blockage.

Testing battery life

When a standard battery is dropped on its negative (flat) side (from a relatively low height) on a hard surface, for example, a solid table and it bounces, the battery is discharged. If the battery does not bounce and simply falls over upon landing, the battery is still good.

Campfire site tips

Chain an old spade to a pole by the fire pit. This way you will always have a tool to spread coals or push logs into the fire. Also, fit a permanent water pipe right next to the fire pit to make it easier and safer to extinguish fires.

Fence fixing tips

Fixing fences on your own will save you a lot of money.

After linking a loose or broken fence line, you will have to retighten the wire.

Distances for laying out a fence

Normally anchor posts are placed 200 metres apart or at corners. Iron Y-pegs are placed 15 metres apart and wire spacers/droppers 3 metres apart in between the iron pegs (four spacers are creating five spaces in between two iron pegs). In some cases where small animals are enclosed for security purposes, the y-pegs can be moved to 10 metres apart with spacers 2 metres apart or closer.

Setting up anchor posts and corner posts

Poles are planted at least 1.5 metres apart and a post is fixed between the two at the top. Thick wire is attached as low as possible on the one post and on the highest point of the other post. The process is repeated in reverse to form a cross.

Remember: Tie the wire to the post furthest away for a tight pull and then tie it to the second post for support. Otherwise, the fence will tug on the second pole which is not supported in the direction of pull.

Posts can also be planted with angled support in the direction of pull.

Producing a two- or three-strand wire tip

If a single strand of wire is not sufficient for your needs there is a solution. Hook or fasten the ends of two or three strands of wire in a table vice and the other ends to a power drill chuck. While pulling the wires tight, power the drill to wind the wires into a braid.

This also works for straightening a single strand of wire or a thin metal rod.

How to mix concrete

Material strength is measured in megapascal (MPa).

One MPa equals 10.1972 kgf/cm2 (kilogram force per square centimetre).

❖ Low-strength concrete = 10 – 19 MPa

Used for foundations and low-wear applications.

Recipe if using 42.5N cement:

1 part cement + 4 parts sand + 5 parts stone

Recipe if using 32.5N cement:

1 part cement + 3.5 parts sand + 3.5 parts stone

❖ Medium-strength concrete = 20 – 29 MPa

Used for home floors and pathways.

Recipe if using 42.5N cement:

1 part cement + 3 parts sand + 3.5 parts stone

Recipe if using 32.5N cement:

1 part cement + 2.5 parts sand + 2.5 parts stone

❖ High-strength concrete = 30 – 35 MPa.

Used for commercial flooring, roads, etc.

Recipe if using 42.5N cement:

1 part cement + 2.5 parts sand + 3 parts stone

Recipe if using 32.5N cement:

1 part cement + 2 parts sand + 2 parts stone

How much concrete do I need for a slab, foundation or pathway?

Use the cubic metre formula: depth (metres) x width (metres) x length (metres) = cubes metres (m^3)

To produce one cube metre (1m^3) of medium strength concrete, using 42.5N strength cement, you will need

6.1 bags cement

0.61 m^3 sand

0.71 m^3 stone

Before pouring the concrete, remove all vegetation from the surface and materials (sand and stone) used as it will rot away and leave a hollow, weak spot.

The more water you use in your mix, the weaker the concrete.

Curing concrete (keeping a project such as a floor moist for as long as possible) strengthens the surface.

Start the curing process as soon as possible. Concrete can be covered with a tarp or plastic sheet to prevent quick evaporation and to protect the surface against elements (rain, hail, etc.) until it hardens.

Clean all equipment as soon as possible after use or clean it continually during the process.

Wet the wheelbarrow before pouring the concrete into it, or it will stick to the wheelbarrow.

Replacing old roof nails with new screws

Replacing old roof nails with new ones is often a futile exercise as you end up with loose-fitting nails. Instead, buy a screw that is slightly bigger than the old nail and fit it with a rubber seal. This screw will grip onto the sides of the old hole and seal the roof again.

Traditional Drilling VS Hammer drilling

Most handheld drills have two settings: One simply rotates the drill bit; the other hammers the drill bit forward as well. Application is straightforward: To drill into cement, brick, plaster or concrete, use the hammer drill setting; to drill through wood, plastic or iron, use the regular drill setting.

Advice: Use the regular drill setting on plaster for the first centimetre before switching to hammer drill. If you start in hammer drill mode, you may chip the painted plaster and leave a rough edge around the hole.

Different drill bits

There are many different types of drill bits for different applications (wood, metal, masonry, tile/glass, etc.).

Wood drill bits

Brad point bits – Their sharp points immediately grip the wood.

Auger drill bits – A screw tip and large spiralling shaft are used to cut larger deeper holes in wood.

Paddle bits – The sharp point makes the hole and guides the bit before the paddle-shaped blade cuts larger holes.

Forstner / Hinge bit – Mostly used to install concealed cupboard hinges.

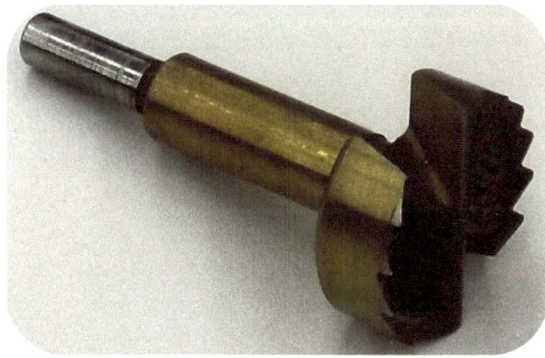

Metal drill bits

High-speed steel (HSS) bits – Used for drilling hard objects such as plastic or steel. Can be used on wood as well.

Masonry drill bits

Their blunt edges, reinforced for the hammering action, are used to drill through plaster, cement, brick and concrete.

Tile and glass bits

This hard, spear-shaped tip enters glass or tile and then enlarges the hole as it goes deeper.

Other types

SDS bits – These drill bits fit into a chuck (a type of drill head) and there are various types available with different attachments.

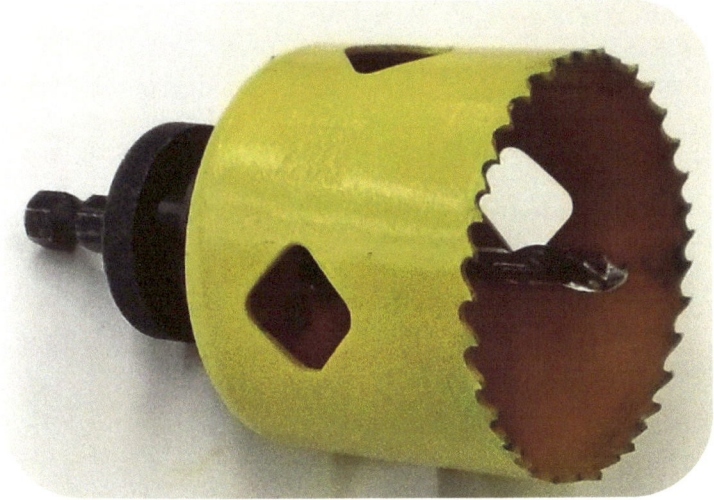

Hole cutter bit – This bit accommodates different circular saw blades that can be screwed on around a normal drill bit. It is used to cut large circles. There are wooden and multipurpose types that can be used for wood, plastic and steel. The normal drill bit in the centre guides the hole cutter keeps it from sliding around on the surface.

Prolonging the life of a drill bit

To prolong a drill bit's life, you need to let it cool down periodically, especially when drilling through metal. Use a spray bottle or dropper to wet the drilling area so that the drill bit can cool down while drilling. Special cooling foam can also be used. Some solid concrete

surfaces can also cause a drill bit to overheat and can benefit from cooling.

Tip for drilling through smooth surfaces, for example, a tile: To keep drill bits from wondering around, apply masking tape over the area before you start drilling.

How to install a window

Measuring a window is the most important part of window repairing.

The first step is to very carefully remove all the old/broken glass pieces along with all the old window putty. Then, measure the width and length of the windowpane opening. You can subtract two millimetres from the measurements, for easier fitting, should the frame allow.

The putty should be kneaded until warm and soft. Add some putty inside the frame then scrape and even it out with a putty knife. Push the new glass into the frame and onto the putty. Level the glass and push firmly. Now push putty into the corners and sides and scrape the putty at an angle. It helps to wet the putty knife with some turpentine to achieve a smooth surface. Scrape off any excess putty from the glass and frame.

Glass in wooden window frames is sometimes fastened with a piece of wood called beading that is nailed to the frame. In this case, you first need to remove the beading before replacing the glass. Once you are done, nail the beading back to keep the window in place.

PHOTO CREDITS

The open source creative commons photos and pictures used are given credit here. No copyright infringement is implied.

Rusty key – Simon Hammond

Measuring tape – Sarahluv

At sign – Howard Lake

Getting the most of money pile – Shiela Martin

First aid kit – Deacon Kevin

Sharps container – Coastal Elite

Report – Got Credit

Emergency – Eadaoin O'Sullivan

Warning - Andrew Klimin

Emergency kit – Pack Config

Team – Madame Furie

Assemble – Pankaj Kaushal

Emergency sign – Marcin Wichary

Dial – Kevin Doncaster

Adhesive bandage – Fraser Graham

EpiPen – Tony Webster

Fire – Vladimir Pustovit

QR – Fabrice de Nola

Snake 161424 – OCV

Drinking water – Geralt

Tap – Matthrum

Tap aerator – Msalguero

Solar water heater – Gmourits

Shower – Erica Palmer

Urinals – Michael Hansen

Buttered bread pudding – Zoyachubby

Tap reseater - Johann de Jager

Terminal connector – Kalhh

Gas leak – James Cridland

Battery loading – Michal Jamro

Concrete mixer – Anaterate

Wood drill augur – Schuetz Medien Design

SDS bit – Bru-no

Drill bit wood – Tookapic

Spade drill – Adersonmrjh

Row of drill bits – Andrew M

Forstner drill – Andrew M

Hole saw – Andrew M

Window restoration – Willie Fogg

Pipe cutter - Byrev

Copper elbow - Byrev

Copper fittings – Eugene DIY Den

PVC glue – Dr Coop

www.ingramcontent.com/pod-product-compliance
Lightning Source LLC
Chambersburg PA
CBHW041537220426
43663CB00002B/60